The ICEA Guide to
Pregnancy
&Birth

ICEA

International Childbirth Education Association

Meadowbrook Press

Distributed by Simon & Schuster
New York

Library of Congress Cataloging-in-Publication Data

The ICEA guide to pregnancy & birth /
by the International Childbirth Education Association.
    p. cm.
  Includes bibliographical references and index.
  ISBN 978-0-88166-572-7
  1. Pregnancy--Popular works.   2. Childbirth--Popular works.
I. International Childbirth Education Association.
  RG551.I34 2011
  618.2--dc22
                    2010046628

Writer: Christine Zuchora-Walske
Editor: Megan McGinnis
Creative Director: Tamara JM Peterson
Illustrator: Susan Spellman
Index: Beverlee Day

Published by Meadowbrook Press, 6110 Blue Circle Drive, Minnetonka, MN 55343

www.meadowbrookpress.com

DISTRIBUTION by Simon and Schuster, a division of Simon and Schuster, Inc.,
1230 Avenue of the Americas, New York, New York 10020

15 14 13 12 11   1 2 3 4 5 6 7 8 9 10

Printed in the United States of America

Dedication

To educators, doulas, and nurses who are passionate about
helping women and their families make informed decisions
about their birth experiences.

And to our clients and patients,
who have given us so much by sharing
those experiences with us.

Acknowledgments

We wish to thank the following for their generous contributions to the creation of this work:

Christine Zuchora-Walske; Megan McGinnis; Jeanette Schwartz, RNC, MA, ICCE/CD; Denise Wheatley, ICEA PCE, Doula, Postpartum Educator, IBCLC; Anne Marie (Dolly) Wagner, BS, ICCE/CD; Michele Peterson, ICD, CD (DONA); Terriann Shell, ICCE, IBCLC; and the ICEA board of directors:

Jeanette Schwartz, president
Denise Wheatley, president-elect
Candy Mueller, secretary
Donyale Abe, treasurer
Connie Bach-Jeckell, director
Michele Peterson, director
Terriann Shell, director
Nancy Lantz, director
Anne Marie (Dolly) Wagner, director
David Feild, executive director

Contents

Introduction

If you're reading this book, chances are you're expecting a baby. Congratulations!

Chances are also good that you're feeling a rush of strong emotions. You might be surprised, happy, nervous, confused, worried, excited, and more. However you're feeling, know that you're in good company. Billions of women have walked this path before you—and millions of women are walking it with you right now.

The act of childbearing hasn't changed since the dawn of humankind. Maternity care, on the other hand, has changed a lot. Societies help women through childbearing in ways that evolve as cultures evolve.

This book aims to help you understand both aspects of childbearing. It explains the physical processes of pregnancy, labor, birth, and postpartum. It also describes modern maternity care options. In the following pages, you'll learn:

- How your baby and your body develop throughout pregnancy
- How to stay healthy and comfortable in pregnancy
- How to choose maternity care, get educated, and make informed decisions
- How to prepare for your baby's arrival
- How your body gives birth and how to cope with each stage of labor
- How to deal with childbirth complications that sometimes occur
- How to prepare for giving birth
- How your body and mind adjust after your baby's birth
- How to care for your newborn
- How your partner can support you—and meet his or her own needs—throughout pregnancy, birth, and postpartum

This book is a project of the International Childbirth Education Association (ICEA). ICEA is a nonprofit organization formed in 1960. Its ultimate goal is the best possible health for mothers and babies. To achieve this goal, ICEA promotes informed decision-making, evidence-based practices, and family-centered care in childbirth.

To make an informed decision about maternity care, you must have access to all information that's relevant to your situation. This information should include the best available research evidence on the benefits and risks of a treatment and its alternatives. You should receive guidance—but not orders—from your caregivers. You should be permitted to make decisions based not only on the information and guidance you receive, but also on your values and personal circumstances.

Each pregnancy, birth, mother, and baby is unique. You can't know in advance how your experience will unfold. But if you arm yourself with solid information from this book, from your caregiver, and from other trustworthy resources, you'll be well equipped to handle any decisions that come along.

Chapter 1

Pregnancy

When you become pregnant, you embark on a journey through many new experiences and responsibilities. All this newness can be exciting—and overwhelming.

You may find it helpful to start your journey by learning as much as you can about pregnancy. Educating yourself can help you feel prepared for both the changes of pregnancy and the choices for maternity care.

This chapter provides a primer on your baby's and your body's development during pregnancy. It offers many ideas to help you stay healthy and comfortable as you and your baby grow and change. You'll also learn the signs of possible danger and what to do if you experience one.

Your Due Date

Most caregivers count the duration of pregnancy in weeks after the first day of the mother's last menstrual period (weeks LMP). Pregnancy typically lasts about forty weeks LMP.

It's important to remember, however, that a due date is only an estimate. Pregnancy is considered at term between thirty-seven and forty-two weeks of gestation, as defined by the World Health Organization. A baby born before thirty-seven weeks is preterm; a baby born after forty-two weeks is postterm.[1] A baby born between thirty-four and thirty-six weeks is late preterm.[2] Less than 5 percent of babies are born on their due dates, half of all babies are born within a week of their due dates, and nearly all (90 percent) are born within two weeks of their due dates.[3] New guidelines recommend using ultrasound before twenty weeks of pregnancy to establish a more accurate gestational age of the baby.[4]

To calculate your due date, count backward three months from the first day of your LMP and add seven days. For example, if your LMP started on July 4, you would count backward three months to April 4. Then you would add seven days to calculate a due date of April 11. Your "due month" would be March 21 to April 25, covering thirty-seven through forty-two weeks LMP.

Stages and Changes of Pregnancy

Pregnancy brings dramatic physical changes in you—and amazing growth and development in your baby. Knowing what to expect during a normal, healthy pregnancy can help you enjoy the experience.

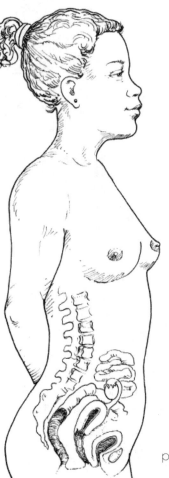

prepregnant

	Stage of Pregnancy	Baby's Development	Maternal Development
Trimester 1 Common symptoms: • frequent urination • abdominal aches or bloating • breast enlarge-ment, tender-ness, tingling, or color changes • constipation • food aversions • nausea or vomiting • metallic taste • fatigue • increased salivation • lightheadedness • increased vagi-nal secretions • weight loss or gain up to 5 pounds (2.3 kilograms)	1 to 6 weeks LMP	• Body is about 0.1 inch (0.3 centimeters) long. • Brain and spinal column start forming. • Gastrointestinal system, heart, and lungs develop. • Heart begins beating.	• Uterus enlarges, and its lining thickens. • Menstrual periods stop. • Chorionic villi (primitive placenta) and amniotic sac form.
	7 to 10 weeks	• Body is about 1 inch (2.5 cm) long. • Eyes, ears, nose, mouth, and teeth buds form. • Limbs start moving. • Fingerprints and genitals appear.	• Uterus is the size of a tennis ball. • Umbilical cord takes shape. • Amniotic fluid fills the amniotic sac.
	11 to 14 weeks	• Body is about 3 inches (7.6 cm) long and weighs about 1 ounce. • Fingers and toes move. • Baby can smile, frown, suck, swallow, and urinate. • Bone cells begin to appear. • Vocal cords are completely formed.	• Placenta is com-pletely formed. • Uterus is the size of a grapefruit and extends just above the pubic bone. • Cervix is about 1.6 inches (4 cm) long, and a mucous plug fills its opening.

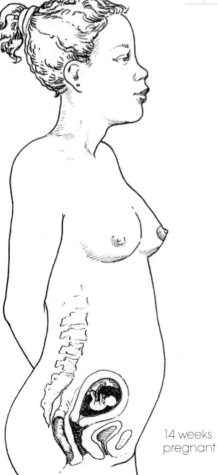

14 weeks pregnant

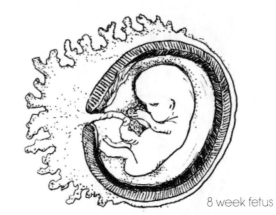

8 week fetus

Notes:

	Stage of Pregnancy	Baby's Development	Maternal Development
Trimester 2 Common symptoms: • increased energy and appetite • decreased nausea or breast tenderness • constipation • food or nonfood cravings • skin changes such as linea nigra or chloasma • nasal congestion • bleeding gums or nose • pelvic joint relaxation • groin pain • leg cramps • weight gain of about 0.8–1 pound (0.4–0.5 kg) per week	15 to 19 weeks	• Body is about 5–6 inches (12.7–15.2 cm) long and weighs about 4 ounces (113 grams). • Lanugo (downy hair) covers the body. • Baby can coordinate movements. • Skin is thin and transparent. • Fingernails and toenails form.	• Uterus reaches 3 inches (7.6 cm) above pubic bone. • Amniotic fluid increases.
	20 to 23 weeks	• Body is about 10–12 inches (25–30 cm) long and weighs about 0.5–1 pound (0.2–0.5 kg). • Baby hiccups. • Hair, eyelashes, and eyebrows grow.	• Uterus extends to navel. • Amniotic sac contains about 2–3 pints (0.9–1.4 liters) of fluid.
	24 to 27 weeks	• Body is about 11–14 inches (28–36 cm) long and weighs about 1–2 pounds (0.5–0.9 kg). • Skin is wrinkled and covered with vernix (pasty protective coating). • Eyes open. • Ears begin hearing. • Meconium collects in the bowel. • Strong grip develops.	• Uterus reaches above navel. • Braxton-Hicks contractions (painless "practice" contractions) begin occurring periodically. • Breasts begin making colostrum.

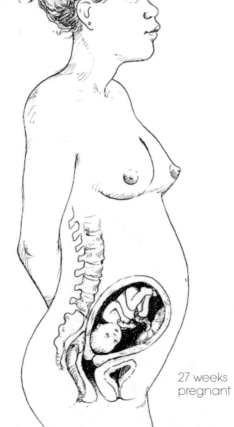

27 weeks pregnant

	Stage of Pregnancy	Baby's Development	Maternal Development
Trimester 3 Common symptoms: • heartburn or indigestion • backache • shortness of breath • clumsiness • rib soreness • difficulty sleeping • urinary urgency • vascular spiders • hemorrhoids • tingling or numbness in hands • varicose veins • stretch marks • abdominal itching • swollen ankles • sweating • anemia • total weight gain of 25–35 pounds (11–16 kg)	28 to 31 weeks	• Body is about 14–17 inches (36–43 cm) long and weighs about 2.5–4 pounds (1.1–1.8 kg). • Body fat develops. • Baby makes breathing motions. • Baby responds to sounds.	• Uterus extends three finger-widths above navel.
	32 to 35 weeks	• Body is about 16.5–18 inches (42–46 cm) long and weighs about 4–6 pounds (1.8–2.7 kg). • Baby sleeps and wakes. • Baby may settle into birth position. • Skull bones are soft and flexible. • Liver stores iron.	• Uterus reaches just below breast-bone and ribs. • Braxton-Hicks contractions increase.
	36 to 42 weeks	• Body is about 19–21 inches (48–53 cm) long and weighs about 6–8 pounds (2.7–3.6 kg). • Skin becomes less wrinkled as body fat keeps developing. • Lanugo disappears. • Lungs mature. • Baby receives antibodies from mother. • Baby assumes birth position. • Body may engage (descend into pelvis).	• Placenta is 6–8 inches (15–20 cm) across, 1 inch (2.5 cm) thick, and weighs about 1 pound (0.5 kg). • Contractions increase. • Cervix ripens (softens) and effaces (thins). • Amniotic fluid decreases.

Full-term

Notes:

Staying Healthy and Comfortable

Tips for a Healthy Pregnancy

Eat Nutritiously

To get the nutrients you and your baby need, eat plenty of fresh fruits and vegetables, whole grains, calcium-rich foods such as low-fat dairy products, and protein foods such as meat, fish, and beans. Vary your diet and drink about 2 quarts (1.9 l) of liquids daily. At first you won't need more food than usual. But by the end of pregnancy, you may need up to 400 extra calories per day.[5] Eating small, frequent meals and snacks can help you control nausea and heartburn and maintain your energy. Talk with your caregiver about a prenatal vitamin supplement.

Gain Adequate Weight

Gaining the right amount of weight during pregnancy can help you and your baby avoid a variety of health problems. If you gain too little, you raise your risk of having a premature baby or one with a low birth weight. If you gain too much, you raise your risk of preterm labor (labor contractions occurring before 37 weeks), gestational diabetes (a condition in which the mother's body has trouble converting food into energy), high blood pressure, or macrosomia (a very large baby).

How much weight should you gain? It depends largely on your weight and height before pregnancy. To assess your prepregnancy weight, visit http://www.cdc.gov/healthyweight and click on "Assessing Your Weight." Then follow the guidelines below. If you are carrying multiple babies, discuss proper weight gain with your caregiver.

- If you begin pregnancy underweight, you should gain 28 to 40 pounds.
- If your prepregnancy weight is in a healthy range for your height, you should gain 25 to 35 pounds.
- If you are overweight, you should gain 15 to 25 pounds.
- If you are obese, you should gain 11 to 20 pounds.

Keep Dental Appointments

You may wonder whether you should postpone routine dental checkups or reschedule necessary dental treatments while you're pregnant. In the past, many pregnant women did so. They and their caregivers worried that common dental procedures and medications might harm a developing fetus.

A recent review of the research shows that dental care—including x-rays and local anesthesia—to prevent, identify, and treat oral diseases is important for the health of pregnant women and their babies. Gum infection, in particular, is associated with preterm labor. Receiving dental care brings no more risk than avoiding dental care.[6]

Use Seat Belts

Whenever you're riding in an automobile or airplane, wear a seat belt. In case of collision, the belt will keep you in your seat. By protecting your body from injury, a seat belt also protects your baby. Position the lap belt low across your hips, below your belly. If the belt has a shoulder strap, use it—don't tuck it behind your back.

Use Approved Medications

When you're pregnant, anything you take into your body can affect your baby. This includes all over-the-counter and prescription medications, herbal remedies, vitamins, and minerals. If you are considering or using any medication, discuss it with your caregiver.

When you and your caregiver discuss whether to use a medication, consider both its possible benefits and its possible side effects. If the benefits outweigh the risks, your caregiver may recommend that you take (or continue taking) a particular medication. If a similar medication with fewer risks is available, your caregiver may recommend switching. If the risks outweigh the benefits, your caregiver may advise you to avoid the medication.

Exercise

If pregnancy is making you feel ill, tired, achy, or cranky, exercise is probably the last thing on your mind. Ironically, exercise might also be exactly what you need to feel better. Regular exercise during pregnancy improves your muscle tone, strength, and stamina. It also minimizes back pain and other common discomforts. It boosts your energy and brightens your mood. It gets your body in good shape for labor, recovery, and parenting a newborn.

To enjoy the benefits of exercise, do a variety of physical activities three to seven days per week. Pay special attention to the muscles in your back, hips, abdomen, and pelvis. Wear cool, comfortable clothing, including a well-fitting bra. Appropriate shoes can help prevent accidents and strained muscles. Begin with warm-up exercises. Drink plenty of water. During exercise, nothing should hurt. You should be able to carry on a conversation while exercising. If you can't, slow down. Cooling down after exercise is important to receive the maximum benefit from your exercise session. Let your caregiver know you plan to exercise and ask him or her for additional safety guidelines.

Don't Smoke, Drink Alcohol, or Use Illegal Drugs

Using tobacco, alcohol, or illegal drugs during pregnancy can cause many serious health problems for mother and baby. The more a pregnant woman uses these substances, the more harm they do. The safest course of action is to avoid all substances not approved by your caregiver for use during pregnancy. If you're having trouble stopping, ask your caregiver for advice and resources to help you quit.

Limit Caffeine

Caffeine is a chemical in many foods and beverages. Coffee, tea, energy drinks, colas, and other soft drinks may contain large amounts of caffeine. Caffeinated drinks provide little to no nutritional benefit. Caffeine can make your heart beat faster, constrict your blood vessels, raise your blood pressure, cause difficulty sleeping, make you urinate more, and pull much-needed calcium from your body. Caffeine can have the same effects on your baby. To avoid potential harm, avoid caffeine during pregnancy. Or limit your daily caffeine intake to less than 200 milligrams. This is the equivalent of one 12-ounce (340 g) serving of coffee per day.[7]

Avoid Infectious Diseases

Some infectious diseases are dangerous during pregnancy. They may cause preterm labor, birth defects, and/or fetal illness. Among these diseases are toxoplasmosis, Lyme disease, rubella, chicken pox, fifth disease, listeriosis, hepatitis, and sexually transmitted infections. To avoid infections, follow these guidelines:
1. Wash your hands frequently each day, especially before eating and after using the toilet.
2. Stay away from sick people as much as possible.
3. To avoid food-borne diseases, wash fruits and vegetables before eating them; skip unpasteurized dairy products; thoroughly cook meat, fish, and eggs; and carefully clean food preparation tools and surfaces.

Avoid Overheating

If you have a high body temperature (oral temperature over 100.4°F or 38°C) during pregnancy, it may be hazardous to your baby. High temperatures can cause birth defects, miscarriage, or neurological problems such as seizures. The risk increases if your temperature rises often, stays elevated for three or more days, or rises very high. To prevent overheating, avoid hot tubs, saunas, full-body heat wraps, and strenuous exercise on hot days. To lower your temperature, drink plenty of liquids and take a lukewarm shower or bath. Take fever-reducing medication only if your caregiver advises you to do so. Seek prompt medical help if your temperature exceeds 102°F (39°C).

Avoid Harmful Chemicals

When you're pregnant, avoid contact with toxic chemicals. These may be household substances or workplace chemicals, or they may be in food. Such chemicals—a long list that ranges from pesticides and paint fumes to lead and mercury—can cause a wide variety of serious problems. These problems include miscarriage, low birth weight, preterm birth, birth defects, developmental delays, and childhood cancers. To avoid exposure to toxins:
- Wash fruits and vegetables to remove herbicides and pesticides. Leave your home during household pesticide application.
- Talk with your employer about limiting your contact with dangerous workplace chemicals.
- Contact your local poison control center to ask about chemicals used in hobbies.
- Have someone else do any house painting. Hire a professional to remove lead-based paint.
- Avoid eating fish that tend to contain high levels of mercury, such as shark, swordfish, king mackerel, and tilefish. Limit your fish intake to one or two meals per week of lower-mercury fish.

Coping with Common Discomforts

Digestive Discomforts

Pregnancy hormones can cause nausea. Also, as digestion slows and baby grows, you may experience constipation or heartburn.

To minimize nausea:

- Eat several small meals and snacks throughout the day, including some protein with each.
- Drink between instead of during meals and snacks.
- Eat a bland snack, such as crackers, before getting out of bed.
- Eat and drink what appeals to you. Avoid what doesn't.
- Avoid smells that nauseate you.
- Sniff peppermint oil, ginger oil, or fresh lemon slices.
- Drink peppermint tea.
- Eat ginger in foods or drink ginger tea or ginger ale.
- Eat foods rich in vitamin B_6 or take supplements (no more than 100 milligrams per day).
- Wear acupressure wristbands.
- If you're taking a vitamin or mineral supplement, take it with food.
- Talk to your caregiver if you have severe vomiting.

To help relieve constipation:

- Exercise regularly.
- Drink plenty of fluids and eat high-fiber foods.
- Try an over-the-counter high-fiber product, such as Metamucil. Avoid laxatives.
- If you're taking an iron supplement, take it with food, try a different brand, or take smaller doses more often throughout the day.

To ease heartburn:

- Avoid fatty, spicy, and gas-producing foods.
- Eat several small meals a day. Drink small amounts of fluid with meals.
- Eat slowly.
- Don't eat just before bedtime.
- Sleep in a reclined—not flat—position.
- Ask your caregiver to recommend an antacid if necessary.

Breast Tenderness

Give your growing breasts the support they need. You may need some larger bras or bras in a different style. Many pregnant women find that stretchy maternity bras, sports bras, or nursing bras are the most comfortable. If aching breasts keep you awake at night, wear a soft, breathable bra while you sleep.

Let your partner know that your breasts are tender. Ask to be hugged gently. Designate a "no touching" zone if necessary.

If breast pain is really getting you down, apply a cool, moist pack or an ice pack to your breasts. To avoid damaging your skin, wrap an ice pack in a light cloth.

Frequent Urination

As your baby grows and your uterus expands, they crowd your bladder. Feeling a frequent urge to urinate is common throughout pregnancy. The best response is simply to urinate as often as you feel the need to do so. You'll be more comfortable overall. Also, by emptying your bladder when it's full, you can help prevent a urinary tract infection.

Notes:

Feeling Dizzy or Light-headed

Lying flat on your back during pregnancy can make you feel dizzy or light-headed. If this happens, lie on your left side or sit up instead. To prevent dizziness or light-headedness while exercising, do not hold your breath. If light-headedness occurs with persistent fatigue, you may have anemia (depleted iron stores). Your caregiver can diagnose anemia with a blood test and recommend ways to increase your iron intake.

Skin Changes

Pregnancy hormones can cause a variety of skin changes. Some of the most common ones are chloasma, linea nigra, vascular spiders, and stretch marks.

Chloasma, or "mask of pregnancy," is a darkening of skin around the eyes. Sun exposure can darken chloasma. You can't prevent it, but you can minimize it by using sunscreen or shading your face from direct sunlight. Chloasma usually disappears after baby's birth.

Linea nigra is a dark line between your navel and your pubic bone. Sun exposure can darken it. It usually disappears after baby's birth.

Vascular spiders may appear on your upper body when tiny blood vessels just under the skin dilate or burst. A vascular spider consists of a small central red bump with reddish "legs" stretching outward. If a facial spider is bothering you, you can mask it with makeup. Vascular spiders usually disappear slowly after baby's birth.

Stretch marks are reddish lines appearing on expanding areas of skin, such as your abdomen, buttocks, breasts, thighs, or arms. Applying lotions or oils may soothe tight or itchy skin. However, research shows that such treatments usually don't prevent stretch marks.[8] The marks typically fade and shrink after baby's birth.

Swollen Feet and Ankles or Varicose Veins

Hormones and increasing body weight can slow your blood circulation during pregnancy. Poor circulation may lead to swollen feet and ankles or varicose veins. Varicose veins are swollen, twisted blood vessels that bulge just beneath the skin. To improve circulation:

- Avoid prolonged standing or sitting.
- Exercise regularly.
- When you're sitting, elevate your feet, rotate your ankles, or rock in a rocking chair. Don't cross your legs at the knees.
- When you're resting, lie on your side or sit with your feet up.
- Do pelvic tilt exercises. Get on your hands and knees. Keep your back straight and your knees slightly apart. Tighten your abdominal muscles, curling your pelvis under and arching your back.

- Walk, play, or swim in deep water for an hour every other day.
- Wear support stockings, especially if you must stand a lot.

Hemorrhoids

Hemorrhoids are varicose veins in the rectum or anus. They may itch, bleed, sting, or ache, especially during a bowel movement. To prevent hemorrhoids and reduce discomfort:

- Prevent constipation.
- Apply witch hazel to the affected area.
- Soak in a warm bath for ten to twenty minutes.
- Avoid heavy lifting.
- Do Kegel exercises. (Without holding your breath, tighten your pelvic muscles as if you're stopping the flow of urine. Hold this muscle contraction for ten seconds. Repeat several times.)

Shortness of Breath

Your growing baby and expanding uterus may be crowding your lungs, causing shortness of breath. If you have this problem while lying down, avoid lying on your back. Instead lie on your side; tilt your body with pillows under one shoulder, hip, and leg; or rest in a semi-sitting position with the help of pillows or a recliner. Exercise can also help maintain good lung function.

If shortness of breath occurs with persistent fatigue, you may have anemia. Your caregiver can recommend ways to increase your iron intake.

Round Ligament Pain

Round ligaments are muscular cords that connect your uterus with your groin (lower abdomen) tissues. When you stand up quickly or when you sneeze or cough, you may stretch your round ligaments too fast, making them reflexively—and painfully—contract. To prevent round ligament pain, move slowly, letting the ligaments stretch gradually. Before sneezing or coughing, bring your thighs closer to your belly to reduce round ligament pulling.

Leg Cramps

Some pregnant women get leg or feet cramps while resting or sleeping. Poor circulation, fatigue, dehydration, pressure on nerves, or mineral imbalance may cause these cramps. To prevent them:

- Eat a balanced diet and drink plenty of water.
- Don't stand on tiptoe or point your toes.
- If you get leg cramps, stretch your calf muscles or hamstrings (the muscles on the backs of your thighs) before bedtime. If you get feet cramps, stretch your feet muscles by flexing your toes.

Emotions

Pregnancy can be an emotional roller-coaster ride. Your feelings may swing from proud to worried, from happy to weepy, from confident to irritable. Moodiness is normal during pregnancy. If you're experiencing mood swings, cut yourself some slack. Remember that you're undergoing a life-changing

Notes:

process that includes major hormonal shifts. Talking with your partner or another loved one can also be helpful. Share your thoughts and feelings and work through them together. If you're finding pregnancy very stressful, take steps to reduce your stress level:

- Try to get adequate sleep at night and rest during the day.
- Set aside time for relaxation with slow breathing, meditation, or listening to soothing music.
- Pamper yourself. Treat your body to a manicure, massage, or facial.
- Do something you enjoy.
- Exercise regularly.
- Eat a balanced diet and drink plenty of water.

Sexuality

Many women experience changes in their sexual relationships during pregnancy. You may sometimes feel too ill, too tired, too big, or too clumsy for intimacy. At other times, you may feel beautiful, ripe, and sexual. You or your partner may worry that sexual intercourse will harm your baby. Your partner may be either turned off or turned on by your changing body. As your pregnancy progresses, your sex life will no doubt have its ups and downs.

If your caregiver has not advised you against sexual activity, you can feel free to follow your libido. It's fine to have as much or as little sex as you desire. Remember that your amniotic sac cushions and protects your baby, and that orgasmic uterine contractions can't harm a healthy pregnancy. If you feel discomfort during sex, try different positions. And it's important to keep communicating with your partner. Working together through the changes in your sexual relationship will help prevent tension between you.

Backache

As your body changes in size and shape, your back will need some special attention. To prevent back pain:

- Practice good posture. If you have good posture, your body is vertically aligned. When you're standing, from the side your ears, shoulders, hips, and ankles form a straight line.
- Use good body mechanics. To get out of bed, roll onto your side, swing your lower legs over the edge of the bed, push yourself to a sitting position, and stand up. To get up from the floor, get onto your hands and knees. Place one foot on the floor in front of you and keep the other knee on the floor. Use your legs to stand up, holding onto your knee or a stable object for balance.
- Avoid heavy lifting. If you must lift something, use your legs instead of your lower back to raise your body. Keep your back straight.
- Do exercises that strengthen your abdominal muscles.
- Do pelvic tilt exercises. (See page 10.)

To relieve back pain:
- Try rest, massage, a warm bath, hot packs, or cold packs.
- Investigate chiropractic therapies.
- Do not take pain medications unless your caregiver recommends them.

Nasal Congestion and Nosebleeds

Pregnancy hormones can cause your nasal membranes to swell and soften, leading to nasal congestion or nosebleeds. To relieve congestion and prevent nosebleeds:
- Blow your nose gently.
- Use saline nasal spray or drops. You can make saline drops at home by mixing 1 cup warm water, ⅛ teaspoon salt, and a pinch of baking soda.
- Consider using a neti pot. A neti pot is a simple device you can use to flush out your nasal passages with a saline solution.
- Run a cool-mist vaporizer in your home to add moisture to the air.
- Dab a little petroleum (or non-petroleum) jelly inside each nostril.
- Make sure you're drinking enough water and getting enough rest.
- Avoid decongestants, antihistamines, and nasal sprays unless your caregiver recommends them. If you have frequent or severe nosebleeds, discuss them with your caregiver.

Domestic Violence

Pregnant victims of domestic violence face a higher risk of several serious pregnancy complications. Domestic violence victims who become pregnant also face a higher risk of death at their partners' hands.[9]

It's normal for couples to argue occasionally. But domestic violence is different from normal tension, and it's never acceptable. If you answer yes to any of the following questions, you may be in an abusive relationship.
- Does your partner constantly put you down?
- Has your partner caused harm or pain to your body?
- Does your partner threaten you, your baby, or other family members?
- Does your partner blame you for your partner's own actions?
- Is your partner growing more violent or abusive over time?
- Has your partner promised not to hurt you again, but continues to hurt you anyway?

No one deserves to be abused. If you're in an abusive relationship, remember that it is not your fault. Then take steps to protect yourself and your baby.

First, confide in someone you trust, such as a friend, a clergy member, your caregiver, or a counselor. Then contact a local crisis hotline, domestic violence program, legal aid service, or shelter for abused women. If you feel isolated or need help finding resources, call the National Domestic Violence Hotline (800-799-7233). This service can provide you with someone to talk to as well as resources to help you toward a safer situation.

Next, make a plan for your safety:
- Memorize the phone numbers of your local police and your caregiver's office in case your partner hurts you. Call 911 if you need urgent help. Get copies of police and medical records in case you decide to file charges against your abuser.
- Collect cash and important documents or items, such as a driver's license, health insurance cards, a checkbook, bank account information, Social

Notes:

Security cards, or prescription medications. Keep these things in one secure place so you can take them with you at a moment's notice.

- Pack a bag with toiletries, a change of clothes, and an extra set of house and car keys. Have someone you trust keep the bag in case you need it.
- Find a safe place where you can stay at any time of day or night.

Warning Signs

About 85 percent of pregnancies are healthy and uncomplicated.[10] But it's important to know the signs of a potential problem. If you experience any of the following symptoms, call your caregiver immediately so he or she can help you assess the situation and, if appropriate, begin treatment promptly.

- **Vaginal bleeding** may be a sign of miscarriage, placenta previa (a placenta lying over or near the cervix), placental abruption (separation of the placenta from the uterus), or preterm labor.
- **Fever higher than 102°F (39°C)** may be a sign of infection.[11]
- **Sudden swelling of your face or hands** may be a sign of preeclampsia. (Preeclampsia is a dangerous condition related to high blood pressure in pregnancy. See page 70 for more information.)
- **Blurred vision, seeing spots or flashes, or blind spots** may be a sign of preeclampsia.
- **Severe or persistent headache, dizziness, or fainting** may be a sign of preeclampsia or ectopic pregnancy (pregnancy implanted outside the uterus).
- **Rapid weight gain** may be a sign of preeclampsia.
- **Pain or burning with urination** may be a sign of a urinary tract infection or a sexually transmitted infection.
- **Abdominal pain** may be a sign of ectopic pregnancy, miscarriage, placental abruption, preterm labor, or an unrelated medical problem, such as appendicitis or gallbladder disease.
- **Vomiting or diarrhea lasting more than twenty-four hours** may be a sign of infection.
- **Major changes in your baby's movement** may be a sign of fetal distress.
- **Persistent abdominal cramping or contractions before thirty-seven weeks** may be a sign of preterm labor.
- **Irritating vaginal discharge** may be a sign of a vaginal infection or a sexually transmitted infection.
- **Pelvic pressure or heaviness** may be a sign of preterm labor.
- **Constant, low, dull backache** may be a sign of miscarriage or preterm labor.
- **Leak or gush of fluid from your vagina** may be a sign of premature rupture of the amniotic sac.

Chapter 2
Getting Off to a Good Start

A pregnant woman's to-do list is long. You have so many choices and preparations to make!

Luckily, pregnancy is rather long, too. As you face the many decisions and tasks of pregnancy, remember that you needn't resolve them all immediately. In fact, you'll probably be better off taking the time to make decisions carefully. And spreading out your to-do list over several months will make it less overwhelming.

Get off to a good start by checking three key items off your list. **Arrange your maternity care. Plan your prenatal education. Learn how to make informed decisions.** This chapter will help you complete these tasks. After that, the rest will follow naturally.

Notes:

Arrange Maternity Care

Check Your Insurance Coverage

Having a baby can be expensive. It's important to understand your health insurance coverage before you try to make decisions about maternity care. Your birthplace and caregiver options depend to some extent on your coverage.

If you have health insurance, find out which facilities and caregivers your policy covers. Find out which, if any, are "in-network" and which are "out-of-network." Your health insurance policy may grant more coverage for some providers (in-network) and less for others (out-of-network).

You should also learn about the extent of your insurance coverage. That is, what specific maternity care (prenatal, labor and delivery, recovery, and new-born care) services does your policy pay for? How much of the cost of each service is covered?

When you enrolled in your insurance plan, you probably received a hand-book explaining your policy in detail. If you don't have a handbook, request one from your insurance company's customer service department. After consulting the handbook, if you don't understand parts of your maternity care coverage, ask a customer service representative for clarification.

If you live in the United States and don't have health insurance, contact your state or county public health department. You may be eligible for Medicaid maternity coverage, a federally funded program available in every state.

Choose a Birthplace

Once you understand your health insurance coverage, you'll know what your birthplace options are. Among these options, choose the one that makes you feel the most comfortable and safe. Choose the one best able to provide the expertise and care you need or want.

Choose your birthplace before choosing a caregiver, if possible. Caregivers generally attend births

Bella Vie Gentle Birth Center

only at specific locations. If you choose your birthplace first, you can narrow your caregiver options to a list of individuals who attend births there.

Hospital Birth

If you are considering having your baby in a hospital, try to learn about the hospitals available to you. If your insurance gives you broad access or you live in an area with many hospitals, you might not be able to investigate all the options. But do check out several of them. Hospital philosophies, policies, and services can differ dramatically.

To learn about a hospital, meet or talk with a hospital customer service representative. Visit the hospital's website. Schedule a tour of the facility. Ask the following questions, as well as any others you may have.

- What level of maternity care do you provide? Do you serve low-risk pregnancies only? Do you offer any specialized care, such as twenty-four–hour anesthesia or laboratory services or a neonatal intensive care unit (NICU)?
- What is your nurse-to-patient ratio during the various stages of labor, birth, and recovery?
- What types of nurses attend women and babies in your maternity department? Are they registered nurses, practical nurses, nursing assistants, or other professionals or paraprofessionals? Are any of them floating or temporary employees?
- Do you encourage the use of birth plans?
- How do you monitor the baby's heart rate during labor?
- Can I move around during labor?
- Do you permit eating and drinking during labor?
- Do most laboring women receive intravenous (IV) fluids?
- What pain relief medications are available? What non-drug pain relief methods do you encourage?
- Do your labor rooms have bathtubs? What are your policies regarding laboring and birthing in tubs?
- Do you limit the number and/or types of support people present during labor and birth? May children be present? Do you welcome doulas? Who may be present for a cesarean birth?
- How long is the typical stay after a vaginal birth? After a cesarean birth?
- Do you support skin-to-skin contact immediately after birth and for the first hour or so after birth?
- Can you please describe the typical procedures that happen right after birth? Where do they happen? Who conducts them? Can my baby remain skin-to-skin while the procedures take place?
- How many room changes will I experience during my stay?
- Can my partner stay overnight?
- What are your visiting hours?
- Does your staff include International Board Certified Lactation Consultants (IBCLCs)? If so, can I call them for advice after I leave the hospital?
- Do you provide any post-discharge follow-up care?

Birth Center or Home Birth

If you are having a low-risk pregnancy, you may consider having your baby at a freestanding birth center or at home. An out-of-hospital birth is a safe and appropriate choice for women who are in good mental and physical health throughout pregnancy; who want consistent personal care during pregnancy, birth, and postpartum; who have access to a well-trained midwife; and who want only necessary interventions during birth.

To learn about a **birth center**, meet or talk with the center's staff. Visit its website. Schedule a tour. Ask the following questions, as well as any others you may have.

- Is this center licensed by the state? Is this center licensed by the Commission for the Accreditation of Birth Centers (CABC)?
- What are the credentials of the center's midwives? Are they certified? By which organization(s)? Are they licensed by the state? How many years of experience do they have?

- Can I meet all the caregivers who might attend my birth?
- Does the birth center offer childbirth education? Classes in newborn care? Breastfeeding? Postpartum adjustment?
- How much do services at this center cost?
- Can you bill my insurance plan directly? Can you make payment arrangements with me, such as a sliding scale or installments?
- What pregnancy conditions would require me to plan my birth at a hospital instead?
- During labor, what situations would require me to transfer to a hospital?
- If transfer becomes necessary, what is the backup hospital? Who are the backup caregivers?
- What is your rate of transfer during labor? What is the most common reason for transfer? What percentage of women who transfer have cesarean sections?
- Could my midwife remain active in my care if I transfer?
- Could you explain how you would handle various emergencies that might happen during labor and birth?
- Under what circumstances would my baby need to be taken to a hospital? Which hospital would it be?
- Who can be with me during labor and birth?
- Do the midwives here routinely provide continuous support during labor? Do you encourage doulas?
- What are your usual practices for monitoring baby's heart rate, movement, eating and drinking, IV fluids, pain relief, use of tubs, birthing positions, and episiotomy?
- Do you encourage the use of birth plans?
- What happens if labor is progressing slowly?
- What would happen if I decided that I want an epidural?
- Do you support skin-to-skin contact immediately after birth and for the first hour or so after birth?
- Can you please describe the typical procedures that happen right after birth? Where do they happen? Who conducts them? Can my baby remain skin-to-skin while the procedures take place?
- Does your staff include International Board Certified Lactation Consultants (IBCLCs)? If so, can I call them for advice after I leave the center?
- How long is the maximum stay after birth? Who can stay with me?
- What follow-up care and support can you provide after I go home?

To help you consider whether **your home** is a good choice of birthplace for you, answer the following questions.

- Do you deeply desire to give birth at home? Does the prospect of birthing at home make you feel safe, comfortable, and reassured?
- Are you willing to educate yourself and take good care of yourself?
- Are you willing to defend your choice to skeptical friends and family members?
- Do you trust your body's natural ability to give birth?
- Are you committed to giving birth without pain medication?
- Are you committed to finding and working with a skilled caregiver who can continually and accurately assess your fitness for home birth?

- Do you understand that if complications arise during pregnancy or birth, you might have to give birth in a hospital? Are you willing to be flexible?
- Are you willing to prepare your home for birth and obtain whatever supplies your caregiver recommends?
- Are you prepared to work with your insurance company for coverage of your home birth and/or to pay for it yourself if coverage is lacking?

Choose a Maternity Caregiver

Once you've chosen a birthplace, you'll know what your caregiver options are. Following is a list of the most common maternity caregivers.

Doctors

- An **obstetrician-gynecologist (ob-gyn)** has graduated from medical school and has three or more years of additional training in women's health, pregnancy, birth, and postpartum. Ob-gyn education focuses on detecting and treating problems. Ob-gyns attend births in hospitals.
- A **perinatologist** is an ob-gyn with additional training and certification in managing high-risk pregnancies and births. Perinatologists treat patients referred by caregivers, such as ob-gyns and midwives, who usually see lower-risk patients. They attend births in hospitals.
- A **family doctor** has graduated from medical school and has two or more years of additional training in family medicine, including maternity care and pediatrics. Family doctor education focuses on the health care needs of the entire family. Family doctors consult with specialists, such as ob-gyns or perinatologists, when pregnancies develop complications. Family doctors attend births in hospitals.
- An **osteopath** has graduated from a college of osteopathic medicine. Osteopathic medicine combines medical testing and treatment with hands-on diagnosis and treatment focusing on the muscles, bones, and nerves. Osteopaths with additional training in obstetrics or family medicine may provide maternity care.

Midwives

- A **certified nurse-midwife (CNM)** has graduated from nursing school, passed an exam to become a registered nurse, and has one or more years of additional training in midwifery. CNMs focus on the needs of healthy women during the childbearing year. They refer to specialists if complications arise. CNMs attend births in homes, hospitals, and birth centers.
- A **certified professional midwife (CPM)** has received training from a variety of sources, including apprenticeship, school, and self-study, and has been the primary caregiver at twenty or more births. A CPM must pass an exam given by the North American Registry of Midwives (NARM). CPMs

Notes:

focus on the needs of healthy women during the childbearing year. They refer to specialists if complications arise. CPMs attend birth center and home births.

- A **licensed midwife (LM)** has completed the educational and apprenticeship requirements of her state and has passed an exam given by the state licensing board. LMs focus on the needs of healthy women during the childbearing year. They refer to specialists if complications arise. LMs attend birth center and home births. Many LMs are also CPMs.

Interviewing a Potential Caregiver

Among the caregivers available to you, choose the one best able to provide the expertise and care you need or want. To learn about a caregiver, visit his or her website. Schedule an informational interview. Ask the following questions, as well as any others you may have. If you're taking medications or have a health problem that might affect the maternity care you need, tell the caregiver during the interview.

- What education, credentials, and/or experience do you have?
- Who provides backup care when you are unavailable?
- Do you handle all your prenatal appointments? If not, who assists you?
- What are the chances you'll attend my birth? Do the caregivers in your group share a similar philosophy?
- Do you encourage the use of birth plans? Will your colleagues respect my birth plan?
- Do you encourage childbirth education?
- Do you welcome doulas?
- What do you think of trying for natural childbirth? How many of your patients attempt natural childbirth? How many succeed? Do you avoid routine interventions if possible? What non-drug pain relief methods do you encourage?
- How often do you use labor induction, IV fluids, artificial rupture of membranes, continuous electronic fetal monitoring, episiotomy, forceps, and vacuum extraction?
- If my baby and I are doing well, can we have skin-to-skin contact for the first hour after birth?
- How many of your clients have cesareans? What can I do to help reduce my chances of needing a cesarean?
- If I develop complications during pregnancy or labor, will you manage my care? If not, to whom will you refer me?
- When and how often will I see you for checkups after birth?

After interviewing a potential caregiver, ask yourself the following questions.

- Did the caregiver seem open, patient, and comfortable with me?
- Did the caregiver respond thoughtfully to my questions and offer additional explanation upon request?

Get Educated

After you've selected a birthplace and caregiver, it's time to look into prenatal education. You are probably already reading books about pregnancy and parenting, researching online, and discussing key issues with your caregiver. Attending prenatal classes is another great way to prepare for the changes and choices ahead.

Prenatal classes provide valuable information that books, websites, videos, and busy caregivers may not be able to offer. Classes can:

- address local practices;
- incorporate the latest research data;
- let you practice what you're learning;
- provide a chance to ask questions;
- supply immediate feedback and advice;
- give you opportunities to make new friends.

Your hospital, birth center, or caregiver's practice may offer classes for expectant families. These classes generally inform parents about the type of care a birthplace or caregiver offers. They may avoid discussing alternatives or controversial topics.

Your local community may offer prenatal education opportunities, too. A college or university, community group, or independent educator may sponsor consumer-oriented classes. These classes generally inform parents about all possible care options and prepare parents to participate actively in making decisions about their care.

Visit the websites or get brochures from all the organizations offering prenatal classes in your area. Some common offerings are childbirth preparation for first-time parents, childbirth refresher courses, preparing for a cesarean or vaginal birth after cesarean (VBAC), sibling education, classes for expectant fathers, prenatal exercise, breastfeeding education, and newborn care classes. Compare your options to decide which classes suit you best.

To help you choose a childbirth class, try to find answers to the following questions.

- Who sponsors the class?
- What background, training, credentials, and experience does the instructor have?
- Does the class cover both normal and complicated birth? Does it teach about comfort measures and natural childbirth techniques as well as procedures and medications? Does it describe disadvantages and risks as well as advantages and benefits of all childbirth options?
- Does the class cover postpartum adjustment, newborn care, development, and feeding?
- When do the classes meet?
- How much do the classes cost?
- What is the maximum number of students per class?
- Is the instructor available for questions outside of class?

Make Informed Decisions

When your caregiver suggests a test, procedure, or treatment, first ask how urgent the situation is and whether you have time for questions, discussion, and contemplation. If the situation is not an emergency, make an informed decision by asking the following key questions.

Use Your B-R-A-I-N

- **Benefits:** What's the problem we're trying to identify, prevent, or fix? How is the test or treatment done? How will it help me and/or my baby? How likely is it to work?
- **Risks:** What risks does this test or treatment bring to me and/or my baby? How would we handle these risks? Does the test or treatment carry other drawbacks, such as additional procedures for safety?
- **Alternatives:** What are my other options? Might another test or treatment work? Can I delay or decline the test or treatment? What are the benefits and risks of the alternatives?
- **Intuition:** What does my gut say?
- **Next steps:** May I have time to think through this decision and discuss it with my family? What happens if I say "no" or "never"? If the test or treatment identifies or solves the problem, what happens next? If the test or treatment doesn't identify or solve the problem, what happens next?

Chapter 3
Preparing for Baby

Now that you've arranged maternity care, looked into prenatal education, and learned about informed decision-making, you're ready for the next step. It's time to prepare for the addition of a baby to your family.

Work Decisions

Soon you'll become a parent. Sometime before your baby's birth—the sooner, the better—think about how your baby will change the way your family earns a living.

Employment

The first decision you face is whether you will return to income-earning work after your baby's birth. If your family needs your income, or if you believe returning to work is a priority in order to preserve your personal or professional well-being, the choice will be clear to you. If your family budget has some wiggle room, if your career has some flexibility, or if you think a change in employment might be the best choice for your family, you can consider other options. For example, you or your partner might stay at home to care for your child(ren) full-time. Or you might eliminate or minimize the need for child care by creative scheduling. One of you might be able to bring your baby to your workplace or work fewer hours, work a compressed week, or work from home.

If you plan to return to your current workplace, you'll need to think not only about the future shape of your job, but also about maternity leave. The length of maternity leave varies. It depends on several factors: the state where you work, the size of your employer's business, how long you've worked for this employer, and the employer's human resources (HR) policies.

Many mothers are required to end maternity leave sooner than they want. Often women feel as if they're just getting comfortable in their new mothering role when they must return to work. Women know that the time they spend with their babies has a big impact on their babies' development, on bonding, and on breastfeeding.

Keep these facts in mind as you plan your maternity leave. Discuss maternity leave with your employer so you'll know what to expect from each other. Explore creative ways to extend your maternity leave beyond the policies outlined in your HR manual. Use every tool at your disposal to maximize your leave. By using some combination of unpaid parental leave, paid parental leave, paid vacation and sick time, and short-term disability leave, you may be able to get more time off—with less financial hardship—than you expected. Remember that it's okay to negotiate. By thinking outside the framework of written policy, you may be able to craft a strategy that meets both your needs and the needs of your employer. In addition, the process will reassure your manager that you take your job seriously and have concrete plans to return.

Child Care

Depending on your family's work arrangements, you may need someone outside your family to care for your baby. In this case, you'll need to search for safe, reliable, affordable child care. A trusted relative or friend might be able to care for your baby

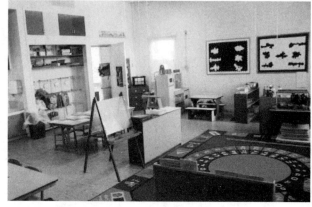

while you and your partner work. You might hire a nanny for your family or share the nanny's services with another family. Or you might choose a home daycare or a child-care center.

Choosing the right child-care provider is a very important and difficult decision. If you're seeking child care outside your circle of friends and relatives, evaluate your options carefully. Use the following steps to guide you.

1. **Plan ahead.** Allow plenty of time for a careful, detailed search. Ask yourself some initial questions: What values do you respect in a child-care provider? Would you prefer a smaller or larger facility? Would you prefer a more structured program or a looser one? What are your needs in terms of location, hours, and cost?

2. **Get a list of providers.** Ask your state or county child-care licensing office for a list of licensed child-care providers in your area.

3. **Contact providers.** Explain your child-care needs—including the age of your child, the schedule you require, and so on—to several providers. Identify at least three providers who meet your basic needs. If you are unsure of the setting you want, identify more. For example, if you're considering both child-care centers and home daycares, identify at least two of each type.

4. **Visit providers.** Visit the child-care providers you've identified. Tour the facilities and interview caregivers. Eliminate any provider that is unwilling to have you visit.

5. **Ask questions and take notes.** Discuss what you want for your child, such as meals, naps, activities, form of discipline, and so on. Briefly explain your values or your parenting style. For questions to ask when evaluating a home daycare or a child-care center, visit http://www.childcareaware.org/en/child_care_101. For questions to ask when evaluating a nanny, visit http://www.babycenter.com/0_nanny-interview-sheet_1450905.bc. Pay close attention to provider responses. Eliminate any provider who is unwilling to answer your questions.

6. **Observe.** Watch and listen closely during each visit. Observe awake, active children to see how the provider interacts with them. Are children engaged and enjoying their activities? Do children have access to age-appropriate toys and equipment? Count the children and adults in the room. Do the child-to-adult ratios meet licensing requirements? Is the facility clean and orderly? Do you hear frantic yelling or enforced silence?

7. **Check references.** Make sure a provider is highly recommended for quality care. Ask a child-care center or home daycare provider for the contact information of past and current clients. Investigate whether the provider has any documented complaints, violations, or lawsuits. Ask a nanny for references from past employers and for permission to run a background check. (For a list of agencies that specialize in screening nannies, see http://www.nanny.org/industrytype/1.)

8. **Compare providers, trust your feelings, and decide.** Study your notes and figure out which provider seems to be the best fit for your family. Pay attention to your feelings and intuition. Negative feelings are usually a good sign that an arrangement won't work out.

9. **Continually evaluate your choice.** After you choose child care, keep assessing it. Visit the provider—both announced and unannounced. Pay attention to your child's daily reactions to child care. Talk to your provider about any concerns you have. Make sure the provider continues to meet your child's needs.

Your Baby's Caregiver

Take a few moments to learn about the types of health professionals who care for babies, then investigate your options. Ask friends, family, and coworkers who cares for their children's health needs. Choose a good fit for your family.

Check Your Insurance Coverage

It's important to understand your health insurance coverage. Check your insurance manual or talk with a customer service representative for clarification on the following issues.

- Which pediatric caregivers your policy covers
- What pediatric services your policy covers, such as well-child visits, vaccinations, circumcision, medications, and hospitalization (At a well-child visit, a caregiver checks your baby's growth, development, and overall health and gives vaccinations as needed.)
- The amount of coverage your policy provides for each service
- Whether copayment is required for each service

If you live in the United States and don't have health insurance, contact your state or county public health department. You may be eligible for coverage under the Children's Health Insurance Program (CHIP), a federally funded program that provides health insurance for uninsured children. Each state sets its own guidelines for eligibility and services. Or the public health department may direct you to low-cost children's health care resources available in your community. For example, your community may be home to a children's health clinic associated with a medical school, a charitable organization, or the health department itself.

Choose a Caregiver

Among the caregivers available to you, choose the one best able to provide the expertise and care you need or want. Following is a list of the most common pediatric caregivers in North America.

- **Pediatrician:** A pediatrician is a doctor who specializes in caring for children's health. He or she has graduated from medical school and has four to eight years of additional training in pediatrics. A pediatrician's examination and waiting rooms are designed specifically for children.
- **Family doctor:** A family doctor has graduated from medical school and has two or more years of additional training in family medicine, including maternity care and pediatrics. Family doctor education focuses on the health care needs of the entire family. Family doctors consult with specialists, such as pediatricians, when children have serious illnesses or injuries.
- **Pediatric or family nurse practitioner:** A pediatric or family nurse practitioner has graduated from nursing school, passed an exam to become a registered nurse, and has one or more years of additional training in pediatrics or family health. Nurse practitioners usually work within a caregiver team. They treat common illnesses and provide well-child care. Nurse practitioners consult with doctors when children have serious illnesses or injuries.

Interviewing a Potential Caregiver

To learn about a caregiver, visit his or her website. Schedule an informational interview. Ask the following questions, as well as any others you may have.

- What education, credentials, and/or experience do you have?
- Who provides backup care when you are unavailable?
- Do you handle all your appointments? If not, who assists you?
- Are you available for consultation by phone or e-mail? Who answers questions for you when you're unavailable?
- Do the caregivers in your group share a similar philosophy?
- How do you feel about breastfeeding? Do you have expertise in breast-feeding? Do you feel comfortable giving breastfeeding guidance? Do you work with certified lactation consultants?
- What are your thoughts on formula feeding?
- What are your thoughts on circumcision?
- What are your thoughts on vaccination? Do you work with parents who wish to selectively vaccinate, delay or space out vaccinations, or refuse vaccination?
- What are your thoughts on using nonmedical remedies to treat minor health problems?
- What are your thoughts on antibiotic use?
- Do you have hospital privileges? If so, where?
- Does your office use electronic charting? (Electronic charting is a secure online system you can use to access your medical records and communicate with your caregiver.)

- Will you be available to examine my baby soon after birth? If not, who will examine my newborn?

After interviewing a potential caregiver, ask yourself the following questions.

- Did the caregiver seem open, patient, and comfortable with me?
- Did the caregiver seem competent, caring, and considerate?
- Did the caregiver respond thoughtfully to my questions and offer additional explanation upon request?
- Did the caregiver's style and philosophy match mine?
- Are the caregiver's hours and location convenient for me?
- Am I comfortable with the caregiver?

Notes:

Notes:

_____

_____

_____

_____

_____

_____

_____

_____

_____

_____

_____

_____

_____

_____

_____

_____

_____

_____

_____

_____

_____

_____

_____

_____

_____

_____

Infant Health Decisions

It's a good idea to make a few key health decisions for your baby before the birth. If you know in advance how you want to feed your baby and how you feel about vaccination, circumcision, and cord blood collection, you can ensure that your baby receives newborn care aligned with your preferences.

Feeding

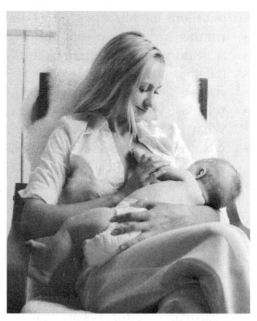

You start feeding your baby early in pregnancy. Throughout pregnancy, your baby gets nutrition, oxygen, and blood from you through the umbilical cord. Your baby is immersed in amniotic fluid, which also provides some nutrients. Everything you eat, drink, smell, and breathe reaches your baby quickly through the umbilical cord and amniotic fluid, so your baby becomes familiar with your daily environment.

When you birth your baby, your body shifts from baby-growing to milk-making. Your blood, the source of prenatal nourishment for your baby, also supplies the raw materials for lactation (milk production). Your milk and your baby share 50 percent of the same genetic material. Your milk provides perfect nutrition, irreplaceable immunity, and familiar smells and tastes. Nothing made from cow's milk, soybeans, or other substances comes close to your milk nutritionally—and nothing else provides any immune protection. Your milk is perfect in quantity; your breasts gradually increase their output as your baby's stomach grows. Your milk is also perfect in quality; it gradually changes during the course of a single feed, throughout the day, and over time to meet your baby's developmental needs. What is more: Lactation and breastfeeding help your body heal and recover normally from childbirth.

Many experts call breastfeeding a baby's "lactational life-support system." All top health experts recommend that babies breastfeed exclusively for the first six months, followed by breastfeeding with complementary foods (family foods or "solid" foods) until babies are at least two years old or for as long after that as mother and baby desire.

Most women truly want to breastfeed. Furthermore, the vast majority of women begin breastfeeding soon after giving birth. More women breastfeed exclusively today than in years past. Women tend to breastfeed longer now, too.

Some medical practices and social barriers, however, prevent women from meeting their own goals. You can take steps now, during pregnancy, to minimize potential obstacles.

- **Learn as much as you can about the mechanics of breastfeeding.** Take a breastfeeding class. Buy or borrow a comprehensive, evidence-based breastfeeding book for parents, such as *The Breastfeeding Book* by Martha Sears, RN, and William Sears, MD. Surf an evidence-based website for parents, such as http://www.kellymom.com. Use what you learn to educate your partner and other loved ones, so they can support you.

Notes:

- **Identify knowledgeable support people.** Join your local La Leche League, a mother-to-mother breastfeeding support organization. Get the names and telephone numbers of lactation consultants who work in your community. Recruit a trusted, experienced friend or relative as a breastfeeding advisor.
- **Plan ahead for work and child care.** If you and your baby will be apart for more than a few hours per day, plan ahead for breastfeeding success. Secure child care that will support your breastfeeding relationship with your baby. Buy or rent a breast pump. Make arrangements with your employer to pump your milk at work. Know the laws protecting breastfeeding rights in your state. For a list of breastfeeding laws in all U.S. states and territories, visit the National Conference of State Legislatures website at http://www.ncsl.org/IssuesResearch/Health/BreastfeedingLaws/tabid/14389/Default.aspx.

Why Is Breastfeeding So Important?

Here's a short list of reasons:

- **Breastfed babies grow and develop normally.** The World Health Organization (WHO) and the American Academy of Pediatrics (AAP) state clearly that breastfed babies' growth and development are the norm. As a group, formula-fed babies are likely to be shorter and fatter and have poorer overall health and development.
- **The composition of human milk promotes optimum brain growth, eyesight development, and nerve function.** Breastfed babies are very alert, take in their world with interest, and thrive mentally.
- **Your milk contains over four hundred components that do double-duty as nutrition and immune protection.** These components affect every part of your baby's body. Most of these components remain active even after you store, freeze, or heat your milk.
- **Your milk adapts during a single feed, changing from lower-fat in the first few minutes to higher-fat near the end of a feeding.** This change helps your baby determine how much to eat, a learning process with lifelong implications.
- **Your milk changes over time, too, matching your baby's developmental needs.** For example, the milk you make at six weeks has more immune components and less calcium than it has at six months, because by six months your baby has a stronger immune system and is beginning to sit up and move around.
- **As a group, breastfed babies get sick less often than formula-fed babies do.** When breastfed babies do get sick, their illnesses tend to be milder than those of formula-fed babies. The immune protection conferred by breastfeeding lasts long after breastfeeding ends—even into adulthood.
- **Breastfed babies are rarely allergic to their mother's milk.** By contrast, dairy products (including formula made from cow's milk) are the most common triggers of children's allergies.
- **Lactation is normal and healthy for you, too.** Breastfeeding helps your body use food efficiently and helps you return to your prepregnancy weight. Breastfeeding usually delays the return of your periods. Breastfeeding helps protect you against reproductive cancers, osteoporosis, and arthritis.
- **Breastfeeding is "green."** It produces no waste and no mess, and it requires no trips to the store. Your body makes milk while you sleep, eat, work, play, and live your life.

Key Facts to Remember

- **Dose matters.** Exclusive breastfeeding is better than partial breastfeeding. Partial breastfeeding is better than none at all. Even one nursing session is important to your baby.
- **Making milk is easy.** You deliver your baby, the placenta comes out, and your milk comes in. If you can gestate, you will lactate. True inability to make milk is extremely rare.
- **Babies are born to breastfeed.** In the first hour after birth, your baby can crawl, wiggle, or scoot to your breast and begin nursing comfortably and well. As you both adjust to your new life together, breastfeeding gets better and better.
- **If you give birth in a baby-friendly hospital or birth center, everything goes more smoothly for you and your baby—regardless of your feeding choice.** A baby-friendly facility is one that has taken special steps to create the best possible environment for successful breastfeeding. It has met criteria set by the United Nations Children's Fund (UNICEF) and WHO. To find a baby-friendly facility in the United States or Canada, visit http://www.babyfriendlyusa.org or http://www.breastfeedingcanada.ca.
- **Your body automatically makes more milk than your baby needs.**
- **The most common problems are insufficient milk** (real or perceived), **breast or nipple pain, disapproval and lack of support, and babies who can't suck normally** (often because of birth interventions, pain medications, or infant illness). These problems are all solvable with prompt, skilled help from a lactation consultant, a breastfeeding peer counselor, a doula with breastfeeding training, your baby's caregiver, or your caregiver.

Breastfeeding Resources Online	
American Academy of Pediatrics: Breastfeeding Initiatives	http://www.aap.org/breastfeeding
Baby-Friendly Hospital Initiative USA	http://www.babyfriendlyusa.org
Breastfeeding Committee for Canada	http://www.breastfeedingcanada.ca
Centers for Disease Control and Prevention: Breastfeeding	http://www.cdc.gov/breastfeeding
International Lactation Consultant Association	http://www.ilca.org
Kellymom: Breastfeeding & Parenting	http://www.kellymom.com
La Leche League International	http://www.llli.org
National Conference of State Legislatures: Breastfeeding Laws	http://www.ncsl.org/IssuesResearch/Health/BreastfeedingLaws/tabid/14389/Default.aspx
UNICEF: Breastfeeding	http://www.unicef.org/nutrition/index_24824.html
United States Breastfeeding Committee	http://www.usbreastfeeding.org
WHO: Promoting Proper Feeding for Infants and Young Children	http://www.who.int/nutrition/topics/infantfeeding/en/index.html

But What If I Don't Want to Breastfeed?

Your milk will still come in. You can express (pump) your milk and give it to your baby with a small cup or a bottle. Alternatively, you can express your milk to avoid discomfort and donate it to a milk bank or throw it away.

If you try breastfeeding first, you can change your mind. If you try formula feeding first, you can't change your mind—at least not easily. If, after careful thought, you're determined to use formula, see Chapter 8 for more information on safe formula preparation and related issues.

Vaccination

What Are Vaccines?

Your immune system protects your body from the millions of dangerous organisms that attack it each day. Several types of white blood cells make up the first line of defense. These cells circulate in your bloodstream along with red blood cells.

An immune reaction begins when microbes (microscopic organisms such as bacteria, viruses, and parasites) enter your body. The invaders can enter through a break in your skin or when you eat, drink, or breathe. Your white blood cells chase down the invaders and destroy many of them.

Suppose the chickenpox virus enters a little girl's body. Her white blood cells help fight and kill much of the virus. She will get sick from the chickenpox. But she will most likely recover if she has a healthy immune system. (Rarely, chickenpox can cause serious illness or death.)

After the girl gets chickenpox, her body's second line of defense kicks into action. Her immune system makes antibodies against the chickenpox virus. Antibodies are proteins that fight attacking microbes. If the chickenpox virus attacks the girl again, her immune system will remember the virus and send anti-chickenpox antibodies to fight off the infection. The girl will not get sick this time because she is immune to chickenpox.

A vaccine is a medication that allows a person to become immune to a disease without getting sick from it. Vaccines are made from killed or weakened microbes. Vaccines are usually injections, but some are oral or inhaled medications. Inside the body, a vaccine stimulates the immune system to make antibodies against a certain kind of microbe.

Suppose that a little boy has never had chickenpox. Instead, he receives the chickenpox vaccine when he is very young. His body makes antibodies against chickenpox. If he is exposed to chickenpox in the future, he most likely will not get sick.

Benefits and Risks of Vaccination

The 1900s spawned a global public health effort promoting vaccination for a variety of diseases. By the early twenty-first century, these efforts led to the near- or complete eradication of several diseases, such as diphtheria, polio, and smallpox, in developed nations.

Vaccination can protect your baby from many diseases. These diseases include hepatitis A and B, diphtheria, tetanus, pertussis (whooping cough), rotavirus, polio, pneumonia, influenza, meningitis, measles, mumps, rubella, and chickenpox. The individual diseases vary in their symptoms and potential severity. But these diseases are all contagious, and all carry some risk of serious illness, lasting health problems, or death.

Because vaccination can slow the spread of disease among both vaccinated and unvaccinated people, most health care experts recommend routine childhood vaccination. Caregivers generally advise that babies and children get vaccinated according to the schedule set—and annually updated—by the U.S. Centers for Disease Control and Prevention (CDC). (For the current vaccination schedule, visit the CDC website at http://www.cdc.gov/vaccines/recs/schedules.) Many child-care centers, home daycares, and schools require proof of certain vaccinations before admitting a child.

Notes:

Vaccination, like any medical procedure, carries risks. Vaccination inserts a foreign substance into the body. Thus, vaccination has the potential to cause an adverse reaction. Severe adverse reactions are rare, but they do happen occasionally.

Also, it's important to keep in mind a few basic facts about vaccines and the diseases they target. Vaccination permanently alters a child's natural immune system. No vaccine is 100 percent effective. Vaccines and the diseases they target are not all equivalent. Some vaccines are more effective than others, and some carry more risks than others. Some of the diseases are fairly common; others are extremely rare. Some of the diseases are more likely to lead to complications or death than others are.

Some parents believe their child's risk of adverse reaction to a vaccination outweighs the risks of the targeted disease. Other parents are hesitant to tamper with their child's natural immune system. Some believe the CDC's vaccination schedule, which recommends multiple simultaneous vaccinations on several occasions, is too taxing for a developing immune system. Others object to vaccination on religious or cultural grounds. Some parents decline vaccination altogether. Others selectively vaccinate or follow a less aggressive schedule than the CDC's.

Vaccination Decision-Making

As a parent, you are responsible for your child's health and well-being. It's both your job and your right to be fully informed about any medical procedure a caregiver recommends for your child, to weigh the benefits and risks, and to provide informed consent or refusal for the procedure. The following tips can help you make informed decisions about vaccination.

- **Thoroughly and objectively investigate individual vaccines.** How did the vaccine develop? What is it made of? What's the purpose of each ingredient? Do you object to any of the ingredients? What side effects and contraindications does the vaccine have? Does your child have any contraindications? Do any of the side effects seem risky for your child? What are the odds of an adverse reaction? What is the available treatment for adverse reactions? How many doses are required? Why? Do some sources object to this vaccine? Why? What studies support the objections? Who funds the objectors? Who funded the studies?

- **Thoroughly and objectively investigate individual diseases.** Who is at risk of catching the disease? What's the treatment for a mild case? What's the treatment for a severe case? What are possible complications of the disease? How often do those complications occur? How can they be prevented? How common is the disease in your area? Has diagnosis or treatment of the disease changed since its vaccine became available?

- **Use current, reliable resources for your research.** For example, read the vaccine manufacturer's inserts. Talk to your baby's caregiver. Visit the CDC website or call the CDC hotline (800-232-7468). Visit the website of the National Vaccine Information Center (NVIC) at http://www.nvic.org. Buy or borrow an evidence-based book such as *The Vaccine Book* by Robert Sears, MD. Contact your public health department for local data on infectious diseases.

- **Do your research in an organized way.** Research vaccines and illnesses in the order they appear on the CDC schedule, so you can make decisions in the order they appear during well-child checkups.

Circumcision

Circumcision is the surgical removal of the foreskin, a layer of skin covering the glans (head) of the penis. Most males who have this surgery undergo it as newborns. The procedure is more complicated and more risky in males over two months old.[1]

In the United States, about 60 percent of boys are circumcised and about 40 percent are intact. The circumcision rate elsewhere in North America, as well as in most of the rest of the world, is lower. The global circumcision rate is about 30 percent.[2]

Parents who choose to have their sons circumcised often do so for religious, cultural, and social reasons. For example, Judaism and Islam both encourage circumcision among their followers. Many non-Jewish, non-Muslim North American parents choose circumcision to follow the norms of their families or communities.

The American Academy of Pediatrics (AAP), The American Academy of Family Physicians (AAFP), and the Canadian Paediatric Society (CPS) agree that circumcision is not essential to a child's health. None of these organizations recommends routine infant circumcision.

The following list of facts can help you decide whether circumcision is the right choice for your baby.[3] After reviewing this list and investigating other resources, discuss this issue with your partner and your baby's caregiver.

Facts about Circumcised Babies

- A newborn feels pain from circumcision and during healing, making anesthesia and pain medication necessary. A very small number of infants may experience side effects or complications of anesthesia or pain medication.
- About 20 to 30 in 1,000 circumcised boys will experience mild to moderate surgical complications, such as irritation of the glans, infection, excessive bleeding, painful urination, or scarring of the urinary outlet.
- About 2 to 3 in 1,000 circumcised boys will experience severe surgical complications, such as hemorrhage or having too much skin removed.
- About 10 in 1,000 circumcised boys will need to undergo a repeat circumcision.
- About 2 in 1,000 circumcised boys will need hospital treatment for a urinary tract infection (UTI) before they are one year old.
- About 1 of every 1 million circumcised males develop cancer of the penis each year.
- No evidence suggests that circumcision prevents prostate cancer or certain sexually transmitted infections.
- International studies link circumcision with a reduced risk of HIV infection. But the CDC doesn't recommend circumcision to prevent HIV infection because circumcision carries risks and provides only partial protection. Circumcised males must still practice other HIV prevention measures, such as correct condom use.

Facts about Intact Babies

- About 7 in 1,000 intact boys will need hospital treatment for a UTI before they are one year old.

Notes:

- About 10 in 1,000 intact boys will need a circumcision later in life for medical reasons.
- About 3 of every 1 million intact males develop cancer of the penis each year.
- Expert opinions conflict over whether intact males experience better adult sexual performance than circumcised males do.

Cord Blood Collection

Cord blood is the blood left inside the umbilical cord and placenta after the cord is cut following a baby's birth. The cord, placenta, and blood are usually discarded after birth. However, the blood can be collected and banked.

Why is cord blood valuable? It is a rich source of stem cells. The stem cells in cord blood are unspecialized blood cells that can develop into any kind of specialized blood cells. Such cells include red blood cells, which carry oxygen; white blood cells, which fight infection; and platelets, which help blood clot. Caregivers can use stem cells to treat people who have blood and immune system disorders.

Cord blood collection is most successful when performed within ten minutes of birth. A member of the caregiver team inserts a needle into a vein of the cord and drains the blood into a sterile collection bag. The caregiver sends the cord blood to a laboratory. The lab analyzes proteins in the blood and tests it for infections and abnormalities. Then technicians freeze the blood and send it to a blood bank for storage. Parents may choose either public or private cord blood banking.

A public cord blood bank provides access to any genetically matched individual who needs treatment. The AAP recommends donation to a public bank for families with no history of blood or immune disorders. Donation is free for donors, but it isn't available everywhere. For a list of participating hospitals, call the National Marrow Donor Program (NMDP) at 800-627-7692 or visit NMDP's website at http://www.marrow.org. Parents who choose to donate cord blood must complete a lengthy health questionnaire.

Cord blood banked at a private facility is available only to family members. A family with a history of blood or immune disorders should weigh the costs and benefits of this option. Private banking typically requires an initial fee of about $2,000, plus an annual storage fee of $100–200. A donor baby who becomes ill usually cannot receive his or her own stem cells. However, another family member often can.

If you are interested in donating cord blood, find out whether your birthplace offers this service. If it doesn't, visit the Parent's Guide to Cord Blood Foundation website at http://parentsguidecordblood.org for information on how to donate cord blood from anywhere in the United States. This website also provides an international list of private cord blood banks. If you choose either donation or private banking, be sure to discuss your decision with your caregiver.

Baby Gear

Immediately after your baby's birth, he or she will need little more than skin-to-skin contact with you and access to your breasts for feeding. Eventually, though, you'll need at least a little baby gear.

Following is a list of baby equipment many parents recommend having. These basic items can help you keep your baby safe and help you care for him or her. If you research and buy or borrow these items now, you'll have them on hand when you need them.

Baby Basics	
Sleeping	bassinet, cosleeper, crib, or hammock bed
	safe sleeping space in your bed or your room
	2 warm sleepers
	swaddling blanket
	2–4 sets of sheets and waterproof mattress pads
	3–6 light blankets
Diapering	supply of disposable diapers or at least 24 cloth diapers and 6–8 waterproof diaper covers
	supply of disposable diaper wipes or at least 12 washable cloth wipes
	diaper disposal bin or diaper pail
	diaper gel to protect skin
	diaper rash ointment
	2–4 waterproof changing pads
	changing table or cushion
Hygiene and health care	baby bathtub
	2–4 soft, hooded towels
	6–8 small, soft washcloths
	cotton swabs
	mild soap or shampoo
	digital thermometer
	baby nail scissors or clippers
Clothing	4–6 climate-appropriate stretch suits with feet
	4–8 undershirts or onesies
	3 pairs of booties or socks
	1 knit hat for indoors and 1 climate-appropriate hat for outdoors
	1–2 climate-appropriate sweaters or jackets
Traveling	car safety seat
	climate-appropriate car seat cover (sunshade for summer, warm blanket or cover for winter)
	carrier for pedestrian travel (sling, front pack, or stroller)
	diaper bag
Nice-to-have items	motion device to soothe fussy baby (exercise ball, swing, or bouncing/vibrating seat)
	dresser
	massage oil
	mobile
	breastfeeding pillow

Notes:

Preparing the Family

If your baby will be joining a family that already includes children or pets, you've got a little extra prep work to do. You'll thank yourself later if you take steps now to help your pet and/or older child adjust to your family's coming addition.

Siblings

Children of different ages react differently to the news of a new baby. The following paragraphs provide tips to help you prepare toddlers, preschoolers, and school-age children. You'll also find tips that may be helpful for a child of any age.

Toddlers

- Remember that your child probably understands more than he or she can express.
- Talk about babies in general, to help your child notice and think about babies.
- Talk about your new baby. Show your excitement about having another family member.
- Read simple picture books about babies and about becoming a sibling.
- Use words such as *sister* and *brother* in everyday conversation.
- Simplify any of the following suggestions for preschoolers to make them appropriate for your toddler.

Preschoolers

- Remember that at this age, your child is very attached to you. Your child may not understand how to share you. He or she may feel threatened by the prospect of a new family member. Your child may also be very sensitive to change.
- Talk to your child about families, babies, and siblings. Point out and discuss families with multiple children. Help your child understand that it's normal for families to have more than one child.
- Read preschool-appropriate picture books about pregnancy and birth, about families having another baby, and about becoming a big brother or sister.
- Enroll your child in a preschooler sibling class offered by your birthplace, your caregiver, or a community organization.
- Link your due date to a special event or season. For example, you might say, "The baby will arrive around the time our tulips bloom."
- Be honest about the changes a new baby will bring. Explain that babies are cute, but also helpless. Talk about what babies can and can't do. Describe typical baby behaviors, such as crying, nursing, and so on.
- Invite your child to help you prepare for the baby's arrival. For example, your preschooler may enjoy shopping with you for baby items.
- If you intend to use some of your child's old things for the new baby, let your child play with or use these items a bit before passing them along.
- Give your child a baby doll so he or she can care for his or her own baby.

- To avoid overwhelming your child, make major changes in your child's routine, such as toilet training or bedroom changes, months before or after the baby's arrival.
- Expect your child's behavior to regress. Understand that regression is a request for attention. Prepare to give your child the attention he or she needs and to give praise when he or she shows maturity.
- Make sure your home is childproofed to minimize your child's risk of having an accident while you're busy tending the new baby.

School-Age Children

- Remember that while an older child might not feel as threatened by a new baby as a younger child might, he or she may resent all the attention a baby gets.
- Read age-appropriate books about pregnancy and birth, about families having another baby, and about becoming a big brother or sister.
- Enroll your child in a school-age sibling class offered by your birthplace, your caregiver, or a community organization.
- Discuss pregnancy and birth. Find out what your child knows, fill in gaps, correct misconceptions, and answer questions. Use correct anatomical terms.
- Be honest about the changes a new baby will bring.
- If the baby's birth will change sleeping arrangements, make changes months before your due date to prevent your child from feeling displaced.
- Make a calendar with your child to count down the days to your baby's birth.
- Invite your child to help you prepare for the baby's arrival. For example, your school-age child may enjoy helping you set up and decorate the baby's room.
- Talk about ways your older child can help you care for the baby. Consider your child's maturity and abilities. For example, he or she might enjoy holding the baby or singing, talking, or reading to the baby.
- Explain rules of behavior around babies, such as always asking permission to pick up the baby and always treating the baby gently.

All Ages

- Tell your child about your pregnancy whenever feels most appropriate to you. If you're vomiting a lot or otherwise feeling miserable during the first trimester, you might tell your child then to reassure him or her that you're not sick. If you're concerned about the risk of miscarriage, you might wait until the second trimester. If you think your child will have difficulty understanding or coping with the long wait for birth, you might wait until your belly starts protruding or until the third trimester. Whatever timing you choose, take care that your child hears the news from you first.
- Talk about your child's babyhood. Look at his or her baby pictures and videos. Recall things your child did as a baby, and contrast them with things your child can do now.
- Have your child visit with a friend's or relative's baby to get a feel for what babies are like.
- Let your child experience the baby in utero. Let your child touch your belly and feel the baby move. Point out when your baby has the hiccups. Invite

Notes:

your child to talk or sing to the baby. Bring your child to a prenatal checkup so he or she can hear the baby's heartbeat.

- Prepare your child for the sequence of events that will happen when your baby is born. (See Chapter 4.)
- Prepare a special gift to give your child when your baby is born.
- Reassure your child that your love for him or her will not change after the baby arrives.
- Plan ahead to spend some time alone with your child each day after your baby is born.

Pets

Dogs and cats, like children, need help adjusting to a new baby. Your pet is used to receiving a certain amount of attention from you. Your pet is also accustomed to a certain routine and environment.

You can't explain things to your pet. But while you're pregnant, you can take the following steps to acclimate your dog or cat to the coming changes.[4] For best results, try to carry out this process at least a few months before your due date.

- Gradually reduce the amount of time you spend with your pet.
- If your pet is particularly attached to you, have your partner develop a closer relationship with your pet.
- Schedule a routine checkup with your pet's veterinarian. Get treatment for any health issues and make sure your pet's vaccinations are current.
- If your pet isn't already spayed or neutered, schedule the procedure to happen before your baby's birth. Sterilized pets have fewer health problems, are calmer, and are less likely to bite.
- If your pet is typically fearful or anxious, or if your pet's behavior includes nibbling, pouncing, or swatting at people, consult with an animal behavior specialist.
- Enroll your pet in a training class so you can learn how to safely and kindly assert your authority and control your pet's behavior.
- Accustom your pet to frequent nail trimming.
- Train your pet to sit or lie calmly on the floor beside you until you invite him or her onto your lap.
- Invite a friend or relative with a baby to visit your home. Supervise the visit carefully.
- Help your pet get used to baby-related noises and movements. For example, play a recording of a crying baby, turn on a mechanical swing, or rock in a rocking chair.
- Carry around a life-size baby doll. Practice routine baby care activities, such as feeding, bathing, diaper changing, walking with a stroller, and so on.
- Apply double-sided tape to furniture you don't want your pet to jump on, such as a crib or changing table. Cats in particular tend to avoid sticky surfaces.
- Install a sturdy barrier if you want to keep your pet out of your baby's room. A safety gate should suffice for non-jumpers; jumpers may require a screen door.
- If you've chosen a name for your baby, say it often in your pet's presence.
- If you know you will be using certain products with your baby, such as lotion or shampoo, put a bit on your skin to familiarize your pet with the new smells.
- If you're still worried about your pet's possible reaction to a new baby, discuss your concerns with your pet's veterinarian and your baby's caregiver.

Postpartum Support

If you're a first-time parent, you may not expect baby care to be very taxing. You may wonder: How hard could it be to care for such a small person? If this baby isn't your first, you know that meeting the needs of a tiny human can use up nearly all the time and energy you have. And the job is complicated by the fact that you're simultaneously recovering from birth and undergoing a big family adjustment.

Your adjustment to life with your new baby will be healthier and happier if you line up postpartum support in advance. Seek out friends with whom you can share empathy and camaraderie. If you don't already have friends or relatives with babies, cultivate friendships through a childbirth or fitness class, a breastfeeding support group, a community parenting program, an online parenting forum, or your place of worship. In addition, recruit people to help you with basic household tasks and baby care for the first several weeks after birth. These helpers might be grandparents, other relatives, friends, coworkers, fellow church members, and so on. Or you might consider hiring a helper.

A hired helper might be a baby nurse, a nanny, a mother's helper, or a postpartum doula. A baby nurse or nanny can take care of your baby while you sleep or do other tasks. A mother's helper can do housework, such as cooking, cleaning, laundry, or babysitting older children, while you care for your baby. A postpartum doula is a person (usually a woman) with training and experience in helping women and their families adjust to life with a new baby. She is knowledgeable about newborns' needs and abilities. She also helps new mothers gain confidence and skill while they breastfeed and bond with their babies.

Hiring a Postpartum Doula

If you are interested in hiring a postpartum doula, ask for recommendations from your friends and relatives, your childbirth educator, and your caregiver. You can also search online at http://www.icea.org/content/member-directory.

Before hiring a postpartum doula, meet with her for a face-to-face interview. The following questions can help you decide whether she is a good match for you and your partner.[5]

- Could you tell me about your education, training, and experience as a postpartum doula?
- What is your philosophy about postpartum support?
- Could we meet before my due date to discuss our needs and your role?
- Can I call you with questions before my baby's birth?
- When do your services begin for a family?
- Do you have backup arrangements with another doula in case you become unavailable? If so, can I meet your backup doula?
- Have you had a background check by law enforcement? If not, may we request one?
- Have you been tested recently for tuberculosis?
- Are your vaccinations—especially DTaP—up to date?
- Are you certified in cardiopulmonary resuscitation (CPR)?
- What is your fee? What does it include? Can you offer a sliding scale? Do you have a refund policy?
- Could you provide references?

Postpartum Support Plan

Use the following worksheet to help you brainstorm options and recruit people who can support you in the weeks and months after your baby's birth.

Basic Needs	Strategies	Names
Rest and sleep	People available to help during the day	1. 2. 3.
	People available to help in the evening	1. 2. 3.
	People available to help at night	1. 2. 3.
Empathy and camaraderie	Friends, neighbors, or relatives with babies	1. 2. 3.
	Opportunities to cultivate new friendships with other parents	1. 2. 3.
Nutritious meals (Weeks' worth of meals needed)	People willing to bring meals	1. 2. 3.
	Dishes we can prepare and freeze	1. 2. 3.
	Healthy, affordable takeout options	1. 2. 3.
Housework	Friends and relatives who can help with basic housework	1. 2.
	People/services who can provide paid household help	1. 2.
	List of household tasks we need done regularly	1. 2. 3.
Breastfeeding support	Supportive friends or relatives who can offer encouragement	1. 2. 3.
	Knowledgeable friends and relatives who can offer advice and answer questions	1. 2. 3.
	Local professional breastfeeding support people, such as doulas or lactation consultants	1. 2. 3.
	Local breastfeeding support groups	1. 2.
Sibling support	People who can spend time with older child and/or take child to school, daycare, or other activities	1. 2. 3.
	Times of day, routines, or special activities to maintain/reserve for older child	1. 2. 3.
	Strategies for blending baby into family calmly and lovingly	1. 2. 3.
Adult time	Responsible, loving relatives and friends available for occasional child care	1. 2. 3.
	Safe, reliable paid child-care options	1. 2. 3.
	Activities that help each parent feel rested and energized	1. 2. 3.
	Activities that help parents reconnect with each other	1. 2. 3.

Chapter 4
Childbirth Stages and Strategies

By the third trimester of pregnancy, you may feel as if you've been pregnant forever. You may have a hard time imagining *not* being pregnant. But sooner or later, one way or another, you and your baby will embark on the journey of birth. This chapter will teach you about the stages of normal childbirth—including strategies for coping with each stage. In this context, the term *normal childbirth* means birth that occurs with no complications or interventions (including medications).

Childbirth is your baby's transition from the small world inside your body to the big world outside your body. Many caregivers discuss childbirth in terms of three stages of labor, plus the events that occur just before and just after labor. **Prelabor** occurs before labor begins. **The first stage of labor** includes early labor, active labor, and transition. **The second stage** includes pushing and birthing the baby. **The third stage** is birthing the placenta. **Recovery** occurs after labor has ended.

Prelabor

As you approach the end of pregnancy, your body undergoes changes to prepare for labor. Together, these changes make up prelabor. Prelabor may last anywhere from a few days to a few weeks.

Descent

In the last month of pregnancy or during early labor, your baby begins to descend into your pelvis. Prelabor descent may occur suddenly or gradually and is common among women pregnant for the first time. It is less common among veteran mothers. Descent is sometimes called lightening or dropping.

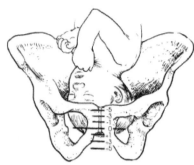

During descent, your baby moves from the highest station to the lowest station. Station refers to the vertical position of your baby in relation to your pelvic bones. Your caregiver can determine your baby's station by conducting a vaginal exam. The highest station is -5. The midpoint of descent is 0 station. A baby at this station is "engaged." The lowest station, just before birth, is +5.

Presentation and Position

Sometime in late pregnancy, your baby will settle into a particular posture and stay more or less that way until labor begins. Babies can settle in a variety of postures. Some lend themselves well to labor and birth; others can make labor longer or more difficult.

Your baby's presentation refers to the part of your baby's body lying over your cervix. The most common and best presentation is vertex. Vertex presentation means your baby is head-down. Less common and more difficult presentations are breech (one foot or both feet presenting), frank breech (buttocks presenting), complete breech (buttocks and feet presenting), and face, brow, or shoulders presenting.

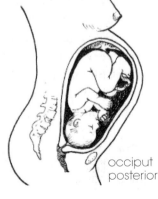

breech

Your baby's position refers to the direction your baby's occiput (the back of his or her head) is pointing. The most common and best position is occiput anterior (OA, or the back of your baby's head against your belly). Other possible positions are occiput posterior (OP, or the back of your baby's head against your back) and occiput transverse (OT, or the back of your baby's head against your side).

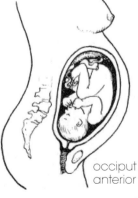

occiput
anterior

occiput
posterior

Cervical Changes

Your uterus is a hollow, muscular organ shaped like an upside-down pear. The cervix is the neck-like opening that lies at the "stem" end of the pear and opens into the vagina. During most of pregnancy, the cervix points toward your back, is firm, measures about 1.2 to 1.6 inches (3 to 4 cm) long, and is closed tightly.

Near the end of pregnancy but before labor begins, your cervix begins to change in preparation for labor. The cervix gradually moves to point toward your belly. The cervix ripens (softens) so that it can change shape during labor. It begins to efface (thin or shorten), changing gradually from a turtleneck shape to crewneck shape. The cervix also starts dilating (opening) at some point while it is effacing.

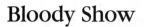
posterior
anterior

If you have a vaginal exam during late pregnancy, your caregiver may tell you if and how your cervix is changing. Caregivers usually express cervical position as "posterior" (pointing toward your back), "midline" (pointing down), or "anterior" (pointing toward your belly). They express ripening as "firm," "medium," or "soft." Effacement is measured in percentages (100 percent indicating complete effacement) or centimeters (indicating the cervical length). Dilation is measured in centimeters, with 10 centimeters indicating complete dilation.

Bloody Show

During most of pregnancy, thick mucus fills the opening of your cervix. This mucous plug seals your uterus shut and protects your baby from infection.

As your cervix effaces and dilates—during either prelabor or labor—the mucous plug loosens and passes out your vagina. The plug may exit your body as a sticky splotch of mucus. Or it may exit little by little, in the form of thin, stringy mucus (that looks and feels like egg white) tinged with blood. This discharge is called bloody show. The blood comes from small blood vessels in your cervix breaking during effacement and dilation.

You may wonder how much blood is normal and healthy. If the discharge is more mucus than blood, you needn't worry. If you have bright red bleeding—enough to soak a small sanitary pad—call your caregiver right away.

Weight Loss

During the last month of pregnancy, your baby will probably gain 1 to 2 pounds (0.5 to 0.9 kg). But your weight may rise only slightly. Or it may stay the same—or even drop by a pound or two (up to a kilogram). This may happen for a variety of reasons:

• Late-pregnancy hormones cause your body to start getting rid of fluid it won't need after it stops growing a baby. Then your body flushes out the excess via perspiration and frequent trips to the bathroom. Less water in your body means less overall body weight.
• You may be spending a lot of time on the toilet for other reasons, too. Your full-term baby is taking up a lot of space in your abdomen and may have begun descending into your pelvis. Both factors mean your bladder is crowded. In addition, late-pregnancy hormones may have loosened your bowels. All these trips to the bathroom free you of ounces.
• You might be burning calories rapidly if you're in nesting mode (see next page).

Notes:

Nesting

Nesting is a late-pregnancy burst of energy. Sometime before labor begins, you may feel a strong urge to prepare your home for your baby's arrival. Many women find themselves zealously cleaning, organizing, shopping, tying up loose ends, or decorating. If you find you're in nesting mode, try not to exhaust yourself. Save some energy for labor!

Fluid Leakage

About 10 percent of pregnant women will leak some amniotic fluid in late pregnancy, before regular contractions begin. You may feel a trickle when you're moving around, or your underwear or bedding may feel damp. Fluid leakage means your amniotic sac has developed a small hole.

Call your caregiver if you think you're leaking amniotic fluid. He or she may want to confirm that it is indeed fluid, and not urine or mucus. Your caregiver may want to prescribe antibiotics if you are at risk for infection.

Nonprogressing Contractions

Near the end of pregnancy, you may experience nonprogressing contractions. A uterine contraction is a tightening of the uterine muscle. Nonprogressing contractions, or prelabor contractions, are ones that occur without changing in strength, length, or frequency. They may occur for a short time or for hours, then disappear or start progressing. (See page 45 for more information on progressing contractions.) Nonprogressing contractions may appear and disappear two or three times over the course of a week. Their job is to promote blood circulation in your uterus, press your baby against your cervix, move your cervix forward, and work with hormones to ripen and efface your cervix.

If you're having nonprogressing contractions, try to be patient. Go about your normal activities. Eat, drink, and occupy yourself with a useful or fun project. Rest often to conserve energy for labor. If your prelabor contractions are strong, use the comfort measures on pages 47–49 to help you cope with them.

The First Stage of Labor

The first stage of labor begins when you start having progressing contractions. It ends when your cervix is completely dilated. The first stage of labor may take a few hours to a couple of days. Caregivers typically divide the first stage of labor into three parts: early labor, active labor, and transition.

Early Labor: What Happens

For most women, the shift from prelabor to early labor is subtle. You may have trouble figuring out if you've crossed that bridge. The two most reliable signs of true labor are progressing contractions and/or rupture of your amniotic sac.

- **Progressing contractions:** Progressing contractions grow stronger, longer, and more frequent over time. To help you figure out whether your contractions are progressing, time them and keep a written record. (See "Early Labor Record" below.) Progressing contractions continue ripening, effacing, and dilating your cervix. They also rotate and push your baby down and out of your uterus. They start at the top of your uterus and move downward. You may feel the contractions starting in your back, then moving to your belly. These contractions will probably be harder to manage than prelabor contractions.
- **Rupture of amniotic sac:** This event is often called rupture of membranes (ROM). When your amniotic sac ruptures, fluid may gush out or you may have a slow, uncontrollable leak. You may hear or feel a distinct *pop!* When a pregnant woman's sac ruptures, many people say her "water broke." ROM usually happens in active labor or later. But some labors start with ROM. If your water breaks first, contractions will probably start within hours. Do not put anything into your vagina after your water has broken. Tampons, douching, fingers, and sexual intercourse increase the risk of infection. You may wear a pad to keep yourself comfortable.

Early Labor Record

Time five or six contractions in a row. Then stop timing them until their pattern seems to change. When the pattern changes, time another five or six contractions. Repeat this process until you can see clearly that your contractions are growing longer, stronger, and more frequent.

Date	Starting Time	Ending Time	Length	Frequency	Other Symptoms or Comments

Notes:

Notes:

Calling Your Caregiver or Birthplace

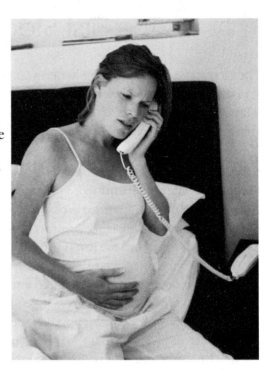

At some point during early labor, you'll probably consider calling your caregiver or going to your birthplace. Your caregiver or birthplace may have given you instructions for what to do at the beginning of labor. Or you may follow these guidelines:

- **If you're a first-time mother, call when:**
  * Your water breaks.
  * Your contractions are five minutes apart, each lasting at least one minute, for a period of one hour and are strong enough that you must focus and breathe rhythmically. (This is called the 5-1-1 rule.)
- **If you've given birth before, call when:**
  * Your water breaks.
  * Your contractions are progressing and you've experienced other signs of labor, such as bloody show or soft bowel movements.
- **If you have a health condition that may complicate labor,** call whenever you think labor has begun.
- Call your caregiver or birthplace at any time if you feel anxious or confused, if you have questions, if you live far from your birthplace or home birth caregiver, or if your caregiver has instructed you to call promptly at the first sign of labor.
- When you call, consult your early labor record and report the following information. The caregiver will use it to determine whether it's time for you to go to your birthplace or for your home birth caregiver to come to your home.
  * Weeks of gestation
  * Length of each contraction
  * Frequency of contractions (minutes from start of one contraction to start of the next contraction)
  * Strength of contractions (whether you can talk through them)
  * How long your contractions have followed this pattern
  * Whether your water has broken and if so, the time of rupture and the amount, color, and/or odor of the fluid
  * Other symptoms, such as bloody show
  * Key info about your pregnancy, such as health conditions or complications

When you arrive at your birthplace or your home birth caregiver arrives at your home, your caregiver may want to confirm that you're in labor. He or she may do a vaginal exam to check your cervical position, ripening, effacement, and dilation. If your water has broken, your caregiver may perform vaginal exams sparingly to reduce the risk of infection.

Coping with Early Labor

Early labor may be long—not to mention unpredictable, frustrating, or confusing. The best way to cope with this phase of labor is to ignore it. Use the following coping techniques to help you stay comfortable and keep a positive attitude.

Stay Home As Long As You Can

If you plan to give birth at a hospital or birth center, you may feel antsy to get there. Resist the temptation to leave home too soon if you have no complications and no history of rapid labor. Here are some good reasons to stay home for a while:

- You are likely to feel far more comfortable at home—with your own tub and shower, a kitchen full of foods you like, and familiar spaces and faces—than you will in a medical setting.
- The longer you spend at your birthplace, the longer your labor will seem, because at your birthplace you can't help but focus on the fact that you're in labor.
- Laboring at a hospital often involves fetal monitoring and IV fluids, both of which limit your mobility. Moving freely is key to staying comfortable and helping labor along.
- Many hospitals restrict food and fluid intake during labor. If you can't eat for a long time, you'll have difficulty keeping up your energy.
- Hospitals are busy places. It can be hard to rest in a noisy, busy place.
- If you want to avoid unnecessary interventions, it'll be easier to do so if you minimize your time at the hospital. Labor is more likely to stall at a hospital because of restrictions on movement and eating. And if your labor stalls at the hospital, you may face pressure to get it going via interventions such as artificial ROM or medication.
- A longer hospital stay means more exposure to potential infections.

Eat and Drink Freely

Research shows that for low-risk laboring mothers, eating lightly and drinking throughout labor as desired carries no risks.[1] To keep up your energy, eat easy-to-digest foods that appeal to you. Many women in labor prefer carbohydrates, such as fruit, pasta, toast, rice, or waffles, and nourishing, soothing liquids such as soup, broth, and herbal tea.

As your labor intensifies, you may lose your appetite. You will still need to stay hydrated and maintain your energy. As early labor shifts into active labor, you may want to sip broth, suck on a Popsicle, or drink water, juice, tea, or sports drinks.

If your caregiver nixes food and fluids, if your labor is very long, or if you're vomiting, you'll probably get IV fluids to prevent dehydration. But your mouth will get dry if you can't drink. Moisten it by sucking on a Popsicle, a sour lolli-pop, or ice chips; by brushing your teeth; or by rinsing your mouth with water.

Use the Toilet Often

A full bladder may slow labor and increase pain, so empty your bladder often. You may also find that you're having a lot of soft bowel movements. This is common in early labor. Your body is making room in your abdomen to facilitate your baby's exit.

Notes:

Distract Yourself

Following are several ideas to keep your mind and body busy during early labor.

- Pack your birthplace bag or prepare your home for home birth.
- Meditate or use guided imagery to help you relax. Meditation is deep concentration on a sound, object, image, movement, idea, or one's breathing in order to promote relaxation, among other goals. Guided imagery is a technique in which one concentrates on a series of mental images in order to relax and improve confidence.
- Have a massage or practice relaxing your muscles. (See page 56 for relaxation techniques.) Contractions may make you tense your muscles. Tension, in turn, amplifies pain. Releasing tension in early labor will give you practice relaxing your muscles in response to contractions. This will come in handy later, when contractions are stronger.
- Take a long, warm shower or bath.
- Fix yourself a tasty snack.
- Take a walk.
- Visit with friends—in person, on the phone, or via online chat.
- Listen to some favorite music.
- Write in your journal, if you keep one.
- Write or e-mail relatives.
- Catch up on household paperwork or organization.
- Watch a movie.
- Dance with your partner.
- Play cards or other games.
- Work on a hobby.
- Launder and sort your baby's clothes.
- Cook one-dish meals to freeze and eat after your baby's birth.

Alternate Rest and Activity

While you're keeping busy, be sure to take regular breaks. Sit or lie down if you get tired, and try to sleep if it's nighttime.

Try Aromatherapy

If you're feeling worried or tense, certain aromas may help you relax and improve your outlook. These aromas include lavender, jasmine, bergamot, neroli, rose, frankincense, clary sage, peppermint, lemon verbena, and spikenard.

Essential oils are the key element of aromatherapy. An essential oil is a pure, plant-derived oil that carries the distinctive scent of that plant. Following are three ways you might use essential oils for aromatherapy in labor:

- Mix a few to several drops of essential oil with about 4 ounces (about $1/2$ cup or 118 milliliters) of carrier oil, such as olive oil or vegetable oil. Ask your partner to use the aromatic oil while giving you a massage.
- Boil 16 ounces (about 2 cups or 0.5 liter) of water. Pour the water into a bowl and add about ten drops of essential oil. The steaming water will heat the oils and make them evaporate quickly, diffusing throughout the room.
- Place a few drops of essential oil on a cotton ball or adhesive bandage and tape the cotton ball to your clothing.

Use Positive Affirmations

These are optimistic statements you can repeat to yourself. Use them as part of a ritual to help improve your outlook. In labor, you might find the following affirmations helpful:

- My body knows how to give birth.
- Birth is safe for me and my baby.
- My baby will be born at the perfect time.
- My baby will find the perfect position for birth.
- I am a strong woman.
- Contractions help bring my baby into my arms.
- Every contraction has a beginning and an end.
- My cervix is opening.
- My breathing gives my baby oxygen.
- I will make the right decisions for my baby.
- I accept the help of others.
- I am surrounded by people who love and respect me.
- I trust my body.
- I am letting go of fear.
- I am competent.
- I am relaxed.

Active Labor: What Happens

You enter active labor when your cervix dilates to 4 or 5 centimeters. At this point, your contractions have probably reached the 5-1-1 mark. They're five or less minutes apart, each lasting at least one minute, for a period of one hour.

Chances are, you're at your birthplace or with your home birth caregiver now. If not, you're probably headed in that direction.

Active labor lasts until your cervix dilates to about 8 centimeters. During active labor, dilation usually speeds up. That is, you will probably dilate from 4 to 8 centimeters faster than you dilated from 0 to 4 centimeters. This acceleration happens because active labor contractions are stronger and more effective than prelabor and early labor contractions.

As active labor progresses, contractions keep growing longer, stronger, and closer together. When your cervix dilates to 6 or 7 centimeters, your contractions may become noticeably more intense.

Transition: What Happens

You enter transition when your cervix dilates to about 8 centimeters. As its name suggests, this is the phase during which you transition from the first stage of labor to the second stage. Your cervix is approaching complete dilation. Your baby is descending into your vagina.

In transition, your contractions are very strong. They last ninety seconds to two minutes and begin every two to three minutes. You may get only a tiny rest between contractions. Because your contractions are so strong, long, and frequent, you may have great difficulty coping with them. You may feel tired, hyper-alert, confused, restless, cranky, hot, cold, fearful, nauseated, shaky, or achy. You may feel the need to "escape" from labor somehow. You may begin feeling the urge to push your baby out.

Transition is a challenging phase of labor. But it is also short. It often lasts less than an hour—including about five to twenty contractions.

Notes:

Coping with Active Labor and Transition

To cope with active labor and transition contractions, you can use any of the methods recommended on pages 47–49 for coping with early labor. You may find that you also need new tools to help you deal with more intense labor. Following are several additional coping methods.

Let Go

Erase expectations about your labor. Release the idea that you can control your progress or your reaction to contractions. Be flexible. Stick with a coping strategy while it works. But when a strategy no longer works, try another.

Remember That Labor Is Finite

No contraction—and no labor—lasts forever. And this part of labor goes faster than early labor.

Keep Your Eyes on the Prize

Bear in mind that every time you experience a contraction, you have one less contraction remaining in your labor. And the harder labor becomes, the closer you are to meeting your baby.

Use the Three Rs

Renowned childbirth educator Penny Simkin teaches that relaxation, rhythm, and ritual are common strategies among women who cope well with labor. Your partner or other support person can help you make the most of these strategies by echoing your behavior; by helping you maintain, adapt, or change your behavior; and by protecting you from disturbance.

- **Relaxation:** You can use a variety of relaxation techniques to help you deal with labor. You might stay quiet, still, unresponsive, and relaxed for all or part of labor. You might move between contractions and relax during them, or vice versa. To learn more about specific relaxation strategies, see pages 56–57.
- **Rhythm:** Rhythmic activity can calm your mind, helping you work with your body. You might breathe, chant, or moan during contractions. You might tap or stroke something or someone. You might rock or dance rhythmically.
- **Ritual:** A labor ritual is repetition of a helpful activity—such as relaxation, breathing, rhythm, movement, or attention-focusing—during contractions. Many women find walking a labyrinth (a maze with many recurring turns) to be comforting during labor. Visit http://labyrinthsociety.org to help you locate a labyrinth in your area.

Comfort Your Body with a Warm Shower or Bath

Caregivers once believed that bathing after rupture of membranes (ROM) leads to infection and other complications. But a recent review of the research shows that immersion in water during labor and birth, even after ROM, is not only safe but also beneficial.[2] The water's warmth, buoyancy, and gentle massage help your mind and muscles relax. Hydrotherapy (water therapy) relieves pain, can lower blood pressure, and may affect labor progress. In early labor, a warm bath can slow down contractions if you need to rest. In active labor, a warm bath often speeds up contractions even while soothing their pain. Here are some tips for showering and bathing in labor:

- **Showering in labor:** To help you rest, lean against the wall or sit on a stool or birth ball covered with a towel. Direct the spray wherever it feels best. Your partner can join you to help support you or to offer extra comfort measures, such as massage.
- **Bathing in labor:** To help you rest, lean against a bath pillow or folded towels. If you're uncomfortable reclining, try lying on your side or kneeling and leaning forward on the edge of the tub. The latter position is helpful for relieving back pain. Keep the water temperature around 98–99°F (36.7–37.2°C). This temperature should feel comfortable for up to ninety minutes. You won't overheat or need to step out of the water to cool off. If you do overheat, your baby's temperature will rise along with yours. Overheating increases your baby's heart rate and stresses your baby's body. If you don't feel relaxed right after you get in the water, be patient. A warm bath may take up to twenty minutes to give you pain relief.

Try an Energy-based Therapy

Energy medicine is a group of therapies proposing that an energy field surrounds and permeates the human body. This energy field is called a biofield. Energy medicine practitioners believe that imbalances in the biofield can cause illness and discomfort and that restoring balance in the biofield can restore health and comfort.

Some energy therapies manipulate the biofield by applying pressure to the body, moving the body, or placing the hands in or through the biofield. Other energy therapies use electricity, magnetism, or sound to manipulate the biofield. Energy medicine includes many different therapies. A few examples are craniosacral therapy, Qi Gong, Reiki, therapeutic touch, healing touch, acupressure, acupuncture, and prayer. If you think that you may use an energy-based therapy in labor, be sure to discuss this beforehand with your caregiver and your birthplace.

Consider Acupressure or Acupuncture

Even if you have never used these therapies before, you may find them helpful in labor. Several studies have shown that acupressure may be effective for decreasing labor pain. Two recent research reviews show evidence that acupuncture is an effective, low-risk option for pain relief.[3]

- **Acupressure:** Pressure on one of two acupressure points can reduce your pain and speed up your labor. These two points are called Hoku and Spleen 6. Hoku is on the back of your hand, at the point where your thumb and index finger bones meet. Spleen 6 is on your leg, about four finger widths above your inner anklebone. Press your thumb steadily into the acupressure point for ten to sixty seconds, then rest for the same amount of time before pressing again. Repeat this pattern three to six times. You can use this method as often as you like during labor. Do not use acupressure on the Hoku and Spleen 6 points before thirty-eight weeks of pregnancy. Doing so can cause contractions and increase your risk of preterm labor.

Notes:

- **Acupuncture:** Acupuncture is the practice of inserting fine needles through the skin at specific points to cure disease or relieve pain. Common sites for acupuncture treatment in labor include the ear, the lower back, the hands, and the feet. This pain relief method requires a trained practitioner. If you think that you may use acupuncture in labor, be sure to discuss this beforehand with your caregiver and your birthplace.

Ask for a Massage

A massage can be helpful in three ways. It distracts your attention from labor. It helps your muscles relax. And the touch of someone you trust can make you feel loved, encouraged, supported, and reassured. Have your birth partner firmly rub, knead, press, or stroke your neck, shoulders, hands, upper back, lower back, hips, thighs, or feet. A tight embrace may also help. On your own, you might try lightly, rhythmically stroking your belly in circles with one or both hands.

Listen to or Make Soothing Sounds

You can use sounds to focus your attention away from your pain. Listen to your favorite music, your partner's voice, or a recording of nature sounds such as rain, rushing water, surf, birdsong, and so on. You can make your own soothing sounds by singing, reciting prayers or poems, chanting, moaning, sighing, or counting your breaths.

Request Transcutaneous Electrical Nerve Stimulation (TENS)

TENS is a device that delivers low-voltage electrical currents through the skin for pain relief. You place four stimulating pads on your back, and then connect them to a battery-operated unit that produces tingling, buzzing, or prickling sensations in the skin. TENS reduces your awareness of pain by increasing your awareness of distracting sensations. TENS may also increase production of endorphins (pain-relieving hormones) in your back. Some women find TENS helpful for relief of labor pain; others don't.

TENS devices are common in North American and U.K. hospitals, but U.S. hospitals may not be accustomed to using them in labor. If you think you might want to try this coping method in labor, you should inquire about its availability beforehand.

Ask for a Sterile Water Block

A sterile water block is a group of four small injections of sterile water into your lower back. The sterile water block relieves back pain by rapidly increasing endorphin production at the injection site. The injection feels like a bee sting at first, but this initial pain lasts less than a minute. The pain relief lasts for one to two hours.

Use a Rebozo

Your partner or caregiver can help you use a rebozo to relieve back pain and improve your baby's position. A rebozo is a traditional Mexican shawl. It is rectangular and is usually about 5 feet (1.5 meters) long. You can use any large piece of fabric—including a folded bedsheet—as a rebozo.

There are many ways to use a rebozo. Ask your childbirth educator to demonstrate the different uses of a rebozo in labor. You can also search the term *rebozo* on the Internet to find examples of rebozo use.

Move Around and Change Positions

If you are willing and able to move around during labor, you can continually find new ways to be comfortable. Movement can accelerate a slow labor by changing the shape of your pelvis and by making the most of gravity to help your baby descend. It can also help you feel more in control of your situation. Following is a list of movements and positions you can try, as well as their benefits.

Action	Description	Image
Standing	This position uses gravity. It helps your baby align with your pelvis. It makes contractions less painful and more productive. If you've been lying down, standing may accelerate labor.	
Walking	This movement offers the same benefits as standing. It also causes continual changes in the shape of your pelvis. It encourages your baby to rotate and descend.	
Standing and leaning forward with support	This movement offers the same benefits as standing, but may be more restful. It also relieves back pain and is a good position for a back massage. It may encourage an OP baby to rotate.	
Slow dancing	This movement offers the same benefits as walking. It is also comforting and is a good position for a back massage.	
Lunge	Lunging widens your pelvis and encourages your baby to rotate. To do a lunge in labor, find a heavy armless chair that won't slide or tip when you lean on it. Stand with your side facing the front of the chair seat. Lift the foot closest to the chair and set it on the seat, pointing your toes toward the back of the chair. Slowly and rhythmically lunge sideways toward the chair by bending your knee and then returning to your starting position. Keep your back straight and upright. Lunge through a contraction, then rest afterward. Repeat for five to seven contractions. If you find lunging uncomfortable, try using the other leg. If it's still uncomfortable, try another position.	
Sitting upright in bed	This position uses gravity to a small degree. It's a good resting position and is safe to use with epidural anesthesia. (See page 78 for more information on epidural anesthesia.)	

Continued on the next page

Notes:

Notes:

Continued from previous page

Action	Description	Image
Sitting or rocking in chair	This position offers the same benefits as sitting upright in bed. It may be more comfortable, and rocking may speed up labor.	
Sitting and leaning forward with support	This position offers the same benefits as sitting upright in bed. It may also relieve back pain and is a good position for a back massage.	
Semi-sitting	This position offers the same benefits as sitting up-right in bed. It's easy to assume and is safe to use with epidural anesthesia. However, it may increase back pain.	
Hands-and-knees	This position helps an OP baby rotate. It can also relieve back pain and take the pressure off hem-orrhoids. It is gravity-neutral and may help slow a rapid labor or reduce a premature urge to push. This position is safe to use with epidural anesthesia.	
Open knee-chest position	This position is useful in early labor to relieve back pain and help an OP baby rotate. In later labor, this position can reduce pressure on a swollen cervix. To assume this position, get on your hands and knees in bed or on the floor. Lower your head and chest to the bed or floor. Scoot your knees back if necessary to raise your hips high in the air. Stay this way for thirty minutes. Ask for support if necessary.	
Side-lying	This position is a good resting position. It can reduce back pain, lower blood pressure, and take the pressure off hemorrhoids. It is gravity-neutral and may help slow a rapid labor. This position is safe to use with epidural anesthesia.	
Semi-prone	This position offers the same benefits as side-lying. In addition, it may help your baby rotate and is safe to use with epidural anesthesia. To get into this posi-tion, lie on your side with your lower arm behind you and your lower leg extended. Bend your upper hip and leg, resting your upper knee on a pillow in front of you. Roll a bit toward your front. Alternate this position with side-lying.	

Breathe Rhythmically

When you do any activity that calls for concentration, coordination, or physical effort, it helps to regulate your breathing. Labor is just such an activity. When you're in labor, rhythmic, focused breathing may help you relax, may distract you from pain, and may actually reduce pain by keeping your muscles well sup-plied with oxygen.

Following are a variety of breathing techniques you can practice before labor and use during labor. Slow breathing and light breathing are the two main techniques. The other techniques combine slow and light breathing.

- **Slow breathing:** This breathing technique helps you stay calm. It's a good one to use when you can no longer walk and talk through your contractions or distract yourself from them. Use it as long as it helps you. To do slow breathing, follow these steps:
  1. When a contraction starts, take a deep breath. Exhale with a sigh to release tension and let your partner know a contraction is beginning.

2. Focus your attention. You can do this by closing your eyes and visualizing an encouraging image; by concentrating on the words of a song, poem, verse, or prayer; by focusing on an image in the room; or by listening to or making soothing sounds.

3. Inhale slowly and quietly through your nose. Exhale completely through your mouth. You might vocalize as you exhale. Keep your shoulders, chest, and belly relaxed as you breathe. Repeat this process five to twelve times per minute throughout the contraction.

4. When the contraction ends, take a deep breath, yawn, or give your partner some other signal to mark the contraction's end.

5. Between contractions, do whatever makes you feel comfortable. For example, you might rest, change position, or take a sip of water.

- **Light breathing:** This breathing technique helps you manage labor pain when contractions are long, strong, and close together. If you simply can't breathe slowly anymore, or if slow breathing is no longer helping you stay calm and relaxed, try light breathing. To do light breathing, follow these steps:

  1. When a contraction starts, take a quick breath in. Then exhale quickly to relax your muscles and let your partner know a contraction is beginning.

  2. Focus your attention.

  3. Inhale and exhale through your mouth, taking a shallow breath every one or two seconds. Inhale quietly, but exhale with a sound. Breathe with the tip of your tongue touching the roof of your mouth just behind your teeth to prevent a dry mouth. Keep your head and shoulders relaxed as you breathe. Continue light breathing throughout the contraction.

  4. When the contraction ends, signal it with a big sigh.

  5. Between contractions, do whatever makes you feel comfortable. For example, you might rest, change position, or take a sip of water.

  6. If your mouth is dry and you're not allowed to drink, suck on a Popsicle, a sour lollipop, or ice chips; brush your teeth; or rinse your mouth with water.

- **Vocal breathing:** This technique simply combines either slow breathing or light breathing with vocalizing. With each exhalation, you sing, hum, chant, sigh, moan, count, or say a word or phrase. If vocalizing helps you cope, your support people should not interfere with you. If necessary at a hospital or birth center, your helpers can shut doors to avoid disturbing others.

- **Contraction-tailored breathing:** This technique works well for contractions that peak slowly. Breathe slowly as a contraction begins. As it strengthens, switch to light breathing. Continue light breathing through the peak of the contraction. As it fades, switch back to slow breathing.

- **Slide breathing:** This technique is a good alternative to light breathing if light breathing is uncomfortable for you or if you have a respiratory condition such as asthma. Inhale slowly and deeply, as if you are doing slow breathing. But when you exhale, do so with three or four puffs of air.

- **Variable breathing:** This is another good alternative to light breathing. Use light breathing for two to four breaths. Then, for one breath, inhale lightly and exhale slowly. On the last exhalation, make a "hoo" or "puh" sound. Repeat the pattern as long as it helps you cope.

Use Relaxation Techniques

You can calm your brain and your body by focusing on different body parts and consciously releasing muscle tension from them. Following are two relaxation techniques you may find helpful in labor.

- **Guided relaxation:** Lie on your side or in a semi-reclined position. Use pillows under your head, limbs, or belly to make yourself as comfortable as possible. Close your eyes and breathe slowly and deeply, as if you're falling asleep. Have your partner read the following script slowly and calmly. If your partner isn't available, listen to a relaxation CD with a similar script.

  1. Inhale slowly and deeply through your nose, all the way down into your belly. Hold the breath for a moment, and then exhale through your mouth. As the air flows out of your lungs, let it carry away all stress and tension.

  2. Once again, inhale slowly and deeply through your nose. Breathe from your belly and fill your lungs completely. Hold the breath for a moment, and then release it through your mouth. Empty your lungs completely when you exhale.

  3. Feel that the tension in your body has begun to loosen.

  4. One more time, inhale slowly and deeply through your nose. Hold the breath for a moment, and then let it go.

  5. Feel your body relaxing more and more deeply with each breath.

  6. Focus on your feet and toes. Inhale deeply through your nose, and as you inhale, gradually curl your toes and tense the muscles in your feet. Hold your breath for a few seconds, and then relax the muscles in your feet and toes as you exhale.

  7. Think about your shins. Inhale deeply through your nose, and as you inhale, flex your feet to tighten your shin muscles. Hold your breath for a few seconds, and then let your shin muscles go limp as you exhale.

  8. Now focus on your thighs. Take a deep breath in and tense your thigh muscles. Hold your breath for a few seconds, and then relax the muscles in your thighs as you breathe out.

  9. Breathe in deeply and gradually tighten the muscles in your buttocks. Hold this contraction for a few seconds, then release your breath and relax your buttocks. Feel the tension leaving your muscles completely.

  10. Inhale deeply and tighten your abdominal muscles. Hold your breath for a moment. Now exhale and let your belly relax.

  11. Think about the muscles in your back. As you slowly breathe in, arch your back slightly and tighten these muscles. Hold your breath for a few seconds. Now exhale and relax your back muscles.

  12. Think about your arms and hands. Breathe in again while clenching your fists and flexing your arm muscles. Squeeze the muscles as you hold your breath for a moment. Now relax your arms and hands and gently breathe all the way out.

  13. Focus on your shoulders and neck. As you inhale deeply, pull your shoulders up toward your ears. Squeeze these muscles as you hold your breath for a moment. Now breathe out. Let your shoulder and neck muscles go limp.

14. Think about your jaw and mouth. Take a deep breath in and press your lips together tightly. Hold your breath for a few seconds and feel the tension in your lower face. Now exhale and let your mouth relax.

15. Focus on your eyes. Breathe in fully. Tighten your upper face muscles by squeezing your eyes shut. Hold this for a moment. Now breathe out and relax the muscles around your eyes. Feel your face softening.

16. Think about your brow and scalp. Inhale deeply and raise your eyebrows as high as you can. Hold this for a few seconds, then exhale and relax your brow.

17. Take one final deep breath in, filling your lungs completely. Hold this breath for just a moment, then release it and relax. Let your exhalation carry away every last molecule of tension.

18. You are now completely relaxed from the tips of your toes to the top of your head. Enjoy this feeling for as long as you like. Take your time. When you are ready, open your eyes.[4]

- **Touch relaxation:** Lie on your side or sit comfortably. Close your eyes. Have your partner use his or her hands to find a tense area on your body, such as your brow, eyes, jaw, neck, shoulders, arms, hands, belly, buttocks, legs, or feet. Your partner should always keep one hand in contact with your body. Your partner stops moving his or her hands when a tense muscle is found. He or she may simply hold a relaxed hand on the area, press firmly on it, lightly stroke the area, or massage it. You use this cue to release the tension and relax into your partner's hand. Imagine the tension flowing out of that body part.

Wear Comfortable Clothing

For a while you'll probably stay in whatever clothing you happen to be wearing when labor starts. But at some point, you may want to change into something more comfortable.

If you're at a hospital or birth center, you might choose a standard hospital gown. But you don't have to wear one if you don't want to. If the staff offers you a gown and you'd rather not wear it, just say, "No, thanks. I'll be more comfortable in my own clothes. I don't mind doing laundry."

Any apparel that allows relatively easy access to your body for monitoring or examination will be fine. You'll probably want your birth clothing to be simple, loose, and soft so you can move about easily and rest comfortably. Also, bear in mind that you may soil your clothing. Choose something that you can launder or that you don't mind staining. You might want to wear a nightgown, a robe, a big comfy T-shirt, a bra or camisole and sarong, or a birth skirt made especially for modesty, comfort, and practicality during labor and birth.

It's okay to strip naked too. If you spend a lot of time in the water, or if you work up a sweat coping with contractions, your birthday suit might be the most comfortable outfit available.

The Second Stage of Labor

The second stage of labor is the pushing stage. It begins when your cervix is fully dilated. It ends when your baby is born.

What Happens

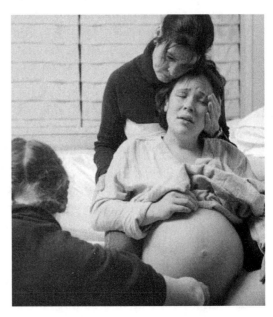

During this stage of labor, your baby gradually exits your uterus, rotates, travels through your vagina, and leaves your body. This process can take anywhere from a few minutes to about three hours. The second stage often lasts longer for first-time mothers than it does for veteran mothers. It has three phases: the latent phase, the descent phase, and the birth phase.

The latent phase is also called the resting phase. Some women get a brief break from contractions during this phase. Once the cervix is fully dilated, the baby's head slips out of the uterus into the vagina. The uterus then fits loosely around the rest of the baby's body. The uterus takes at least a few minutes to shrink a bit and tighten snugly around the baby. In some women, this adjustment may take ten to twenty minutes. The latent phase doesn't occur in all labors. It may be very quick—or nonexistent—if the baby is already very low in the pelvis or is descending rapidly.

When the uterus has adjusted around the baby, it starts contracting again, and the descent phase begins. During this phase, your baby assumes an occiput anterior position (head facing your belly). Little by little, your baby's body exits your uterus and travels through your vagina. Powerful contractions and the sensation of pressure in your vagina create a strong urge to push your baby out. The pushing urge feels somewhat like a need to have a bowel movement. You may involuntarily grunt or hold your breath and bear down. As the descent phase progresses, your perineum bulges, your baby's head inches downward, and your vagina opens each time you push. After each push, your baby's head retreats a little—but not all the way. A push has the effect of two steps forward and one step back.

At some point, you'll push and your baby's head won't retreat. This is the beginning of the birth phase. Your vaginal opening will stretch as wide as it possibly can, causing a burning feeling. Many women call this feeling the "ring of fire." When this occurs, your baby is crowning. His or her head is about to be born. First the crown of your baby's head emerges from your body. Then your baby rotates one-quarter turn, and one shoulder emerges. Then the rest of your baby's body is born. Your caregiver, your partner, and/or you may catch the baby.

Managing the Pushing Stage

You may wonder how to cope with second-stage contractions. And if this is your first baby, the task of pushing your baby out may seem daunting. Use the following techniques to help you push effectively and stay as comfortable as possible.

Spontaneous Pushing

Spontaneous pushing is pushing only when your body involuntarily bears down. This is the best strategy to use if your labor is proceeding normally. Spontaneous pushing is the most efficient way to use your energy. In addition, this method gives your vaginal opening time to stretch gradually, which in turn reduces the risk of tearing or bruising. And because spontaneous pushing doesn't require lengthy breath holding, you and your baby stay well supplied with oxygen.

During the second stage of labor, you'll probably feel three to five strong pushing urges during each contraction. Each urge typically lasts five to seven seconds. Here's how to work with these urges:

1. When a contraction starts, use slow breathing or light breathing to cope with the pain.
2. As the contraction strengthens, continue breathing rhythmically until you no longer can because you feel an irresistible urge to push.
3. When you feel the urge to push, do so. You might hold your breath while you bear down. Or you might inhale, and then slowly exhale by grunting or vocalizing as you push.
4. Bear down for as long as you feel the urge. Relax or bulge your perineum while you're pushing.
5. When the urge to push passes, breathe rhythmically until you feel another urge or until the contraction ends.
6. When the contraction ends, take a couple of relaxing breaths. Then rest in a comfortable position until the next contraction.

Directed Pushing

Directed pushing is bearing down when someone tells you to. It is less effective and more stressful for you and your baby than spontaneous pushing. But directed pushing may be necessary if spontaneous pushing isn't working, if your caregiver or birthplace requires directed pushing, or if you've had pain medication. Epidural and spinal anesthesia reduce—and sometimes eliminate—the urge to push and the ability to spontaneously bear down. (See page 78 for more information on pain medications.) Here's how directed pushing works:

1. When a contraction starts, use slow breathing or light breathing to cope with the pain if necessary. If you're not feeling pain, simply take a few deep breaths.
2. When your caregiver tells you to push, inhale and hold your breath. Curl forward, tuck your chin to your chest, and tighten your abdominal muscles.
3. Bear down for as long and as hard as your caregiver tells you to. Relax or bulge your perineum while you're pushing.
4. Stop pushing when your caregiver tells you to. Exhale, then breathe rhythmically or take a few deep breaths until your caregiver tells you to push again or until the contraction ends.
5. When the contraction ends, take a couple of relaxing breaths. Then rest in a comfortable position until the next contraction.

Movement and Positions

If you are willing and able to move around during the pushing stage, you can continually find new ways to be comfortable. Movement can change the shape of your pelvis and make the most of gravity to help your baby descend. It can also help you feel more in control of pushing. Following is a list of movements and positions you can try in the second stage of labor, as well as their benefits.

Action	Description	Image
Standing	If you've been lying down, this position may increase your urge to push. It uses gravity and makes contractions less painful and more productive.	
Side-lying	This position lets your sacrum (a large, triangular bone at the base of the spine) shift to make a wider opening for your baby. It is a good resting position. It takes the pressure off hemorrhoids. It is gravity-neutral and may help slow a rapid birth. This position is safe to use with epidural anesthesia.	
Sitting upright in bed	This position uses gravity to a small degree. It's a good resting position and is safe to use with epidural anesthesia.	
Sitting on toilet	This position offers the same benefits as sitting upright in bed. It also helps you push effectively because it reminds you of bearing down to have a bowel movement.	
Semi-sitting	This position offers the same benefits as sitting upright in bed. It's easy to assume and is safe to use with epidural anesthesia. It is a common birthing position, so many caregivers feel comfortable with it. However, it may increase back pain.	
Hands-and-knees	This position can take the pressure off hemorrhoids. It is gravity-neutral and may help slow a rapid birth. This position is safe to use with epidural anesthesia.	
Squatting	This position uses gravity and widens the outlet at the bottom of your pelvis. It may help a slow or difficult second stage and may increase the urge to push.	
Lap squatting	This position offers the same benefits as squatting, but it takes less effort and is easier on the knees and ankles. It is also comforting. However, this position might not be possible if you are much heavier than your partner. Here's how to do a lap squat: Have your partner sit on an armless, sturdy chair. You sit on your partner's lap, facing and embracing your partner and straddling his or her lap. Your partner embraces you and sits up straight. During a contraction, your partner spreads his or her thighs, letting your bottom dangle between them. Between contractions, your partner brings his or her thighs together, lifting you up.	

Action	Description	Image
Supported squat	This position offers the same benefits as squatting, but it takes less effort, is easier on the knees and ankles, and is comforting. It allows greater mobility of the pelvis than any other position and eliminates external pressure. It also lengthens your trunk, giving your baby room to maneuver. However, this position requires significant strength and stamina in your partner. Here's how to do a supported squat: During a contraction, you lean back against your partner. Your partner places his or her forearms under your armpits and holds your hands, supporting all your weight.	
Dangle	This position offers the same benefits as the supported squat, but it's easier on your partner. Here's how to do a dangle: Your partner sits on a high bed or counter with thighs spread and feet supported. You stand between your partner's legs, draping your arms over your partner's thighs. During a contraction, you dangle between your partner's legs, taking all the weight off your own legs. Your partner, meanwhile, grips your trunk with his or her thighs.	

Water Birth

If you spend the end of the first stage of labor immersed in water, you may want to stay in the water for the second stage. Or you may be planning to birth your baby in the water. Many parents choose water birth because they believe it provides babies a gentler transition to life outside the uterus. Water birth also tends to reduce medical interventions.

A recent review of the research shows no evidence that birthing in water increases any risks for the mother or the baby.[5] In fact, research suggests that in low-risk women whose caregivers follow professional water birth safety guidelines, water birth can reduce the risk of serious tearing, the need for pain medications, the amount of maternal blood lost, and the risk of infant complications right after birth.[6]

If you desire a water birth, you will need to work with a caregiver who is experienced in this practice. Water birth is commonly available at birth centers and home births. Many hospitals also offer water birth. However, be sure to verify that this option is available at your birthplace before you make plans to birth your baby in water.

Homeopathic and Herbal Remedies

Homeopathic and herbal remedies are both forms of alternative medicine. Many midwives are experienced in using such remedies. Ask your caregiver if he or she has concerns about homeopathic or herbal remedies before you use them.

Although homeopathy is unsupported by scientific evidence, most medical experts consider homeopathic remedies safe—with rare exception. One type of homeopathy often used in childbirth is arnica, which is made from a plant in the sunflower family. A midwife may administer arnica tablets during the second stage of labor to reduce cervical and perineal swelling.

Ginger root is a common herbal remedy used in childbirth. The root may be shredded, wrapped in a warm washcloth, and positioned over the vaginal opening to reduce swelling during the pushing stage. Many mothers say it not only gives comfort, but also smells good.

Notes:

Notes:

The Third Stage of Labor

The third stage of labor is the delivery of the placenta. It begins with the birth of your baby and ends when your placenta exits your body. This stage usually lasts about ten to thirty minutes.

What Happens

After your baby is born, contractions stop for a few minutes. Then they start up again. The job of third-stage labor contractions is to separate your placenta from your uterus. These contractions are usually milder than second-stage contractions.

At this point, you may be physically and emotionally spent—or preoccupied with your baby—so your caregiver will probably talk you through the process of delivering your placenta. He or she may instruct you to bear down a few times until the placenta emerges.

Some caregivers actively manage the third stage in an effort to prevent postpartum hemorrhage (heavy bleeding). Active management may include abdominal massage and/or Pitocin to stimulate contractions. (Pitocin is an artificial hormone that stimulates contractions. See page 77 for more information.) Active management may also include gentle pulling on the umbilical cord to aid the placenta's delivery.

During the third stage of labor, your baby has his or her first experiences outside the womb. Right after birth, your baby's skin may look a bit blue. After your baby begins breathing, his or her skin takes on a normal color. The skin may be covered with vernix, blood, and/or mucus. Ideally, your caregiver leaves any vernix on your baby's skin for at least a little while. Research shows that vernix helps newborn babies adapt to a dry environment and helps prevent dehydration.[7] In addition, vernix contains antibacterial properties that help protect newborns against dangerous infections.[8]

Your caregiver should dry (but not bathe) your baby and place him or her skin-to-skin with you immediately after birth. You and your baby should be covered with a warm, dry blanket. This practice is the best way to keep newborns warm and to encourage early breastfeeding. Most healthy babies can clear their own airways and need no suctioning.

Within one minute after birth and again at five minutes after birth, your caregiver checks your baby's condition using a method called the Apgar assessment. Your caregiver evaluates your baby's muscle tone, heart rate, reflexes, skin color, and breathing, giving your baby a score from zero to two in each category. (See the scoring guidelines on page 63.) The sum of these scores is your baby's Apgar score. A score of seven or higher indicates that your baby is doing well. A score of six or lower signals that your baby may need closer examination or medical help. Your caregiver can conduct the Apgar assessment while you're holding your baby.

Category	2 points	1 point	0 points
Activity (muscle tone)	Active movement	Arms and legs flexed	Limp body
Pulse (heart rate)	More than 100 beats per minute	Fewer than 100 beats per minute	Absent
Grimace (reaction to something placed in nose)	Sneezing, coughing, pulling away	Grimacing	No reaction
Appearance (skin color)	Normal all over	Normal except hands and feet	Bluish, grayish, or pale all over
Respiration (breathing)	Good, crying	Slow, irregular	Absent

At some point during the third stage of labor, your baby's umbilical cord will be cut. Your caregiver first clamps the cord in two places. Then he or she—or you or your partner—cuts between the clamps. The timing of this procedure, as well as your baby's position during the procedure, can affect your baby's blood volume and iron stores. If your baby's birth was uncomplicated and your baby is doing well, cord cutting may occur at least two minutes after your baby's birth and after the cord stops pulsating. Your baby should be lying on your abdomen so he or she is at the same level as your placenta. If your baby is in distress, has a short cord, or is wrapped tightly in the cord, your caregiver may choose to cut the cord sooner.

Coping with the Third Stage

Third-stage contractions are usually milder than second-stage ones. And you may be so overcome with emotion, relief, or fatigue after your baby's birth that you barely notice the contractions that follow. But some women find this stage challenging. If this is the case for you, breathe rhythmically or use relaxation techniques to help you cope (see pages 54–57).

Recovery

After labor has ended, you enter the recovery stage of childbirth. Recovery starts after you deliver your placenta. It ends when your condition is stable. This stage may last anywhere from one to several hours, depending on what happened during your labor.

For most mothers and babies, recovery includes several common experiences and procedures. The following paragraphs describe these common threads.

Your Early Postpartum

Perineum

After you've pushed out your placenta, your caregiver checks your vagina and perineum. He or she looks for tearing or bleeding.

If you have a significant tear or if you had an episiotomy (a surgical incision to enlarge your vaginal opening), your caregiver stitches shut the tear or incision to help it heal. Your caregiver administers a perineal block before stitching.

A perineal block is a single injection of anesthetic in your perineum to numb it. The injection stings, but the stitching should be painless. Your caregiver skips this step if you had epidural or spinal anesthesia during labor or if you received a perineal block before having an episiotomy.

If you didn't tear or have only a small tear, you won't need stitches. But your perineum may be swollen or bruised. An ice pack on the area can reduce swelling and pain.

Uterus

As soon as you've expelled your placenta, your uterus starts returning to its normal size. This process is called involution.

To achieve involution, your uterus continues to contract. These contractions, sometimes called afterpains, should not be severe. But they can be uncomfortable. Some women say they feel like strong menstrual cramps. Slow, rhythmic breathing can help you cope with them.

In addition to shrinking your uterus, postpartum contractions close off the blood vessels that were attached to your placenta. In this way, involution prevents postpartum hemorrhage.

Your caregiver will feel your abdomen frequently to make sure that your uterus is firm—a sign that contractions and involution are occurring. If your uterus is soft and relaxed, you or your caregiver can massage it firmly to stimulate contractions.

Lochia

Lochia is a vaginal discharge that begins immediately after childbirth and lasts for four to six weeks. It contains blood, mucus, the tissue that lined your uterus during pregnancy, and various fluids that helped your body grow a baby. Once your baby is born, your body no longer needs all this extra tissue and fluid, so it passes out through your vagina. Postpartum contractions begin this process.

Over the weeks, lochia should change in color from red to brown or pink to yellow or white. It should also decrease in quantity. You'll need to wear maternity pads at first to absorb the heavy flow. As postpartum progresses, thinner pads will suffice. You should not use tampons during this period, because they increase your risk of infection. If your lochia develops a foul odor, it may be a sign of infection, and you should inform your caregiver about it.

Urination

In early postpartum, your body expels extra fluids not only through lochia, but also through perspiration and urination. Many women sweat heavily and urinate a lot during the first days after birth.

But during the first few hours after birth, you may have difficulty urinating. This difficulty may be a result of tearing, bruising, or swelling. Or it may be a side effect of pain relief medications used during labor.

To solve this problem, you can try the following tips. If you can't urinate after trying these strategies, consult your caregiver.

- Drink plenty of fluids.
- Relax or bulge your perineum while you're using the toilet.
- Pour warm water over your perineum while you're trying to urinate.
- Try to urinate while showering.
- Smell peppermint essential oil while trying to urinate.

Eating and Drinking

Once you enter the recovery stage, you may realize that you are terribly hungry or thirsty. Labor is hard work. No doubt you used a lot of energy to birth your baby. In addition, you may have missed a meal or two. You may not have felt like eating during labor, or your eating and drinking may have been restricted.

If you're at a hospital, tell the staff that you would like to order a meal or a snack. If you're at home or at a birth center, have your partner fetch you whatever sounds good to eat and drink.

Your Baby's First Hours

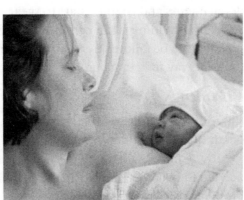

Skin-to-Skin Contact

Skin-to-skin contact between you and your baby immediately after birth—or as soon as possible—helps your baby adjust to life outside your body. It provides several important benefits. For example:

- It keeps your baby at the perfect temperature, helps your baby breathe easily, and stimulates a period of alertness.
- It provides your baby an environment that feels, smells, and sounds safe and familiar while he or she experiences the big new world.
- It gives you and your baby an opportunity to get acquainted. You can easily gaze into each other's eyes; touch, smell, and hear each other; and begin the process of bonding.
- It regulates your hormones and your baby's hormones for the journey ahead.
- It encourages an interest in breastfeeding while your baby is still alert and awake. Most babies are ready to nurse within twenty minutes to one hour after birth. After a few hours, your baby will likely fall into a long, deep sleep.

Skin-to-skin contact between your baby and your partner is beneficial, too. It can strengthen your partner's bonding with your baby, boost his or her confidence as a parent and participation in caretaking, and increase closeness between you and your partner.

Routine newborn procedures need not interfere with skin-to-skin contact. Most of these procedures can take place while you or your partner is holding your baby.

Newborn Examination

Although your baby has already had an Apgar assessment, he or she needs a closer examination, too. When examining your baby, your caregiver will:

- Measure your baby's length, head circumference, and chest circumference;
- Weigh your baby;
- Take your baby's temperature;
- Listen to your baby's heart rate and breathing;
- Check the condition of your baby's various body parts, such as the ears, jaw, chest, breasts, shoulders, arms, legs, hips, and belly.

Throughout the recovery period, your caregiver will periodically recheck your baby's vital signs. He or she will observe skin color, heart rate, breathing, blood pressure, and temperature.

Security

If you give birth in a hospital or birth center, your birthplace should have a policy to ensure your baby's security. This policy should outline procedures for clearly identifying your baby, for preventing kidnapping and accidental baby switching, and for responding to a missing infant.

At most hospitals, newborns and their parents receive matching ankle- and wristbands. In addition, hospitals typically obtain newborn footprints as another means of identifying babies. Hospitals usually limit access to their maternity departments and require staff to wear distinct, official identification badges.

A freestanding birth center may use hospital-like security policies. Or its policies may be tailored to its smaller size, staff, and patient load. At any birthplace, the best way to keep your baby safe is to keep him or her with you at all times.

Vitamin K

Vitamin K is a nutrient the human body needs in order for blood clotting to occur. People produce vitamin K with the help of bacteria in their intestines.

In the first few days of life, newborn babies do not yet have the bacteria needed to make vitamin K. To enhance blood clotting and prevent bleeding problems, most caregivers recommend vitamin K supplements for newborns.

Two methods of vitamin K supplementation are available. A single intramuscular injection shortly after birth is the most efficient, reliable, and common method. Oral vitamin K is also available. A baby receives a dose at birth followed by weekly or daily doses for about one month after birth. This method is effective when performed reliably, but it places the burden on parents to give repeated doses.

Hepatitis B Vaccine

Hepatitis B is an illness caused by a blood-borne virus. The virus infects the liver and causes symptoms such as nausea, weakness, and jaundice. This infection can also lead to serious liver diseases, such as cirrhosis and liver cancer.

Hepatitis B spreads via blood and other bodily fluids. The most common transmission routes are intravenous drug use and sexual activity. However, a baby can catch the virus during birth if his or her mother is carrying it. Some mothers carry the virus without symptoms and thus don't know they are carriers. In addition, hepatitis can spread between family members within households through saliva or by contact with broken skin.

For these reasons, caregivers recommend that newborns receive an intramuscular hepatitis vaccine shortly after birth. Caregivers also recommend a second injection at one to two months and a third dose at six to eighteen months.

Eye Care

If your vagina harbors sexually transmitted bacteria such as Chlamydia or gonorrhea, that bacteria could infect your baby's eyes, possibly causing blindness. To prevent this problem, your caregiver applies antibiotic ointment to your baby's eyes during the recovery period. Because this treatment blurs your baby's vision, it should not take place during the first hour, when your baby is very alert and wants to gaze at you.

Chapter 5

Complications
and Interventions

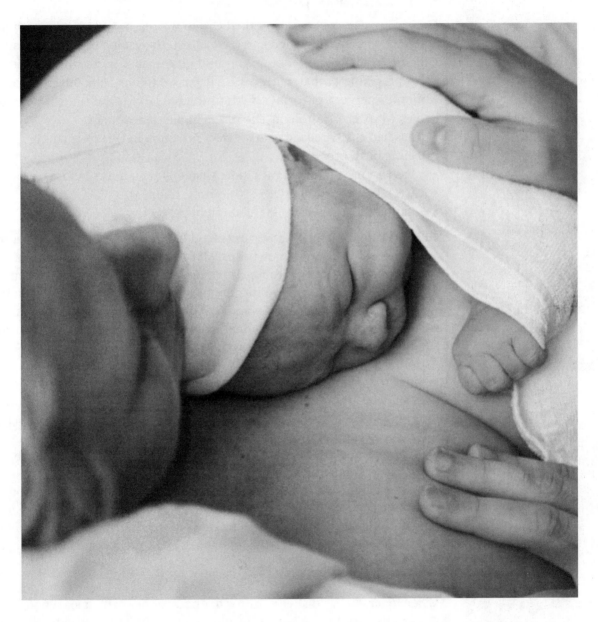

Occasionally childbirth doesn't go as expected. In this chapter, you'll learn about possible complications and medical interventions that can occur during labor and postpartum.

Conditions That Complicate Labor

Some pregnant women develop conditions that can significantly influence labor. These complications include Group B streptococcus, gestational diabetes, low amniotic fluid, placenta previa, placental abruption, pregnancy-induced hypertension, and breech presentation.

Group B Streptococcus

Group B streptococcus (also called Group B strep or GBS) is a bacterium that about 25 percent of women carry, usually in the vagina or rectum. Many adult GBS carriers have no symptoms or mild illness, such as a urinary tract infection.

A pregnant woman with GBS may pass it to her baby during childbirth. About 0.5 percent of women with untreated GBS at the time of birth have babies who get sick from it. The risk is higher if a woman:

- has had a GBS-related urinary tract infection in this pregnancy;
- gives birth prematurely;
- has rupture of membranes more than eighteen hours before birth;
- has fever above 100.4°F (38°C) during labor; or
- has had a baby with GBS infection before.

GBS can cause pneumonia, sepsis (blood infection), or meningitis (central nervous system infection) in newborns. Most infected babies recover with the help of antibiotics; however, 3 to 5 percent die. Between 20 and 30 percent of GBS-infected babies who develop meningitis suffer lifelong neurological damage.[1]

Most caregivers screen women for GBS between thirty-five and thirty-seven weeks of pregnancy. The screening involves swabbing the vagina and anus and sending the sample to a laboratory for testing.

A caregiver may administer IV antibiotics during labor if a woman tests positive for GBS, if she has any of the risk factors mentioned above, or if her GBS status is unknown. Treatment is most effective when it begins at least four hours before birth. The caregiver monitors the baby closely for signs of infection after birth.

This treatment is very effective. It reduces the risk of newborn GBS infection from 0.5 percent to 0.025 percent.[2]

Some caregivers and parents object to the common treatment protocol described above. Only a tiny fraction of babies born to GBS carriers get sick, but all of the mothers and babies treated get exposed to the risks of antibiotics, such as allergic reactions, yeast infections, and drug-resistant bacteria.

Gestational Diabetes

When a person has diabetes, his or her body either can't make enough insulin or can't use insulin effectively. Insulin is a hormone produced by the pancreas. It enables the body to metabolize carbohydrates, or turn them into energy.

Gestational diabetes is diabetes that develops during pregnancy. About 1 to 20 percent of pregnant women develop gestational diabetes, depending on the population.[3] A woman faces a higher risk for gestational diabetes if she has had gestational diabetes before, is older than twenty-five, is overweight, has a family history of diabetes, has had a very large baby in the past, has a history of polycystic ovarian syndrome, has glucose in the urine, or is of African American, Native American, Asian, Hispanic, or Pacific Island ancestry.[4]

Untreated diabetes during pregnancy can cause high levels of sugar in a pregnant woman's blood. High blood sugar, in turn, raises the risk of:

- miscarriage;
- urinary tract infection in the mother;
- preeclampsia in the mother (see page 70);
- too much amniotic fluid, which increases the risk of premature labor and birth;
- cesarean birth (see page 82);
- macrosomia (a very large baby);
- newborn complications, such as low blood sugar, breathing problems, or jaundice (see page 111);
- birth defects;
- preterm birth;
- stillbirth; and
- obesity later in the child's life.[5]

Most caregivers use a blood test to screen for gestational diabetes between twenty-four and twenty-eight weeks of pregnancy. If your screening shows high blood sugar, your caregiver will confirm that you have gestational diabetes by conducting another blood test. New recommendations for screening and diagnosis of gestational diabetes were accepted by the American Diabetes Association (ADA) in 2011 and are currently being evaluated by the American Congress of Obstetricians and Gynecologists (ACOG).

Many women who have gestational diabetes can control their blood sugar levels by eating a carefully planned healthy diet and by exercising. Some women must take insulin medication. All women who have diabetes during their pregnancy must monitor their blood sugar several times per day.

Gestational diabetes usually goes away after birth. About 67 percent of women with gestational diabetes develop it again in future pregnancies. About 50 percent of women with gestational diabetes develop diabetes later in life.

Low Amniotic Fluid

Low amniotic fluid (also called oligohydramnios) occurs in about 4 percent of pregnancies. Its causes include birth defects in the baby, a health condition in the mother (such as high blood pressure), ruptured membranes, and a pregnancy lasting two weeks beyond the due date. Low amniotic fluid can occur at any time, but it usually happens in the last trimester of pregnancy.

In the first and second trimesters, low amniotic fluid can lead to lung and limb defects. It raises the risk of miscarriage, preterm birth, and stillbirth. In the third trimester, low amniotic fluid can lead to poor growth, muscular and skeletal defects, and underdeveloped lungs in the baby. It raises the risk of umbilical cord compression and cesarean birth. (See page 82.)

If your caregiver suspects that you have low amniotic fluid, he or she may order an ultrasound to check your fluid level. If your fluid is low, your caregiver will take steps to prevent complications. These steps depend on how low the fluid is, how far along your pregnancy is, and the health status of you and your baby. In general, you can help by eating a nutritious diet, drinking plenty of water, resting adequately, not smoking, watching your blood pressure, taking only approved medications, and promptly reporting signs of preterm labor.

Notes:

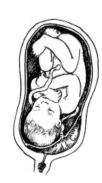
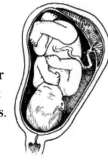

Placenta Previa

In a woman who has placenta previa, her placenta lies dangerously low inside her uterus—completely or partially covering her cervix. Placenta previa is a rare condition. It happens in less than 1 percent of pregnancies.

If you have placenta previa, your caregiver will diagnose it via ultrasound in late pregnancy. As birth approaches and cervical changes occur, you may experience vaginal bleeding. If you do, let your caregiver know right away. Depending on the severity of your condition, your caregiver may recommend that you avoid sex or exertion, may put you on bed rest, or may hospitalize you.

With placenta previa, it is not safe to birth your baby vaginally. You and your caregiver will plan a cesarean birth. (See page 82.) A planned cesarean for placenta previa typically takes place after thirty-six weeks but before labor starts.

Placental Abruption

In a woman who has placental abruption, her placenta partially detaches from her uterus in late pregnancy or during labor. Placental abruption, like placenta previa, is a rare condition. It happens in about 1 percent of pregnancies.

Symptoms of placental abruption include pain in the abdomen or lower back, uterine contractions, and vaginal bleeding. If you experience vaginal bleeding, let your caregiver know right away. Bleeding from a placental abruption can be severe, posing a risk of major blood loss to the mother and oxygen deprivation to the baby.

If you have a placental abruption, your caregiver will monitor your blood pressure and your baby's heart rate to learn how the abruption is affecting you and your baby. Depending on the severity of your condition, your caregiver may recommend bed rest or may hospitalize you. If your bleeding is severe or if your baby's heart rate suggests distress, and if your baby has a good chance of surviving an early birth, your caregiver may perform an emergency cesarean.

Pregnancy-Induced Hypertension, Preeclampsia, and Eclampsia

Pregnancy-induced hypertension (PIH) is a condition in which a pregnant woman develops high blood pressure (several readings over 140/90) after twenty weeks gestation. PIH is more common than placental complications. It happens in about 10 percent of pregnancies in the United States.

PIH is dangerous because it can reduce blood flow to the uterus and placenta, as well as to the other organs of the body. Reduced blood flow can deprive the baby of oxygen and nutrients, cause growth problems, or damage organs.

Left untreated, PIH can worsen into preeclampsia. Preeclampsia is a condition that occurs only during pregnancy. It happens in 5 to 8 percent of pregnancies.[6] Its symptoms include high blood pressure; protein in the urine; sudden swelling in the hands or face; rapid weight gain; headache; changes in or problems with vision; and pain in the stomach, the right side, the shoulder, or the lower back.

Preeclampsia is a nonspecific condition. It doesn't always produce symptoms, and its cause is unknown. Preeclampsia is dangerous because it can progress rapidly, causing placental abruption, eclampsia, or HELLP syndrome. Eclampsia is a life-threatening condition characterized by seizures, stroke, and/or coma. The acronym *HELLP* stands for **h**emolysis (the breaking open of red blood cells), **e**levated **l**iver enzymes (indicating liver damage), and **l**ow **p**latelet count in the blood (which can lead to hemorrhage).

Giving birth is the only cure for PIH. If you have PIH, your caregiver will carefully watch your baby's well-being and will frequently monitor your blood pressure and urine. If your blood pressure is not severely high, and if it stays stable, you may be able to carry your baby to term. PIH often gets worse over time. If you develop preeclampsia, your caregiver may advise you to avoid exertion, may put you on bed rest, may hospitalize you for close observation, or may prescribe medications to lower your blood pressure or to prevent seizures. If preeclampsia becomes severe, your caregiver may recommend labor induction (see page 74) or a planned cesarean. To figure out how soon an induction or cesarean can safely occur, you and your caregiver must consider your health, your baby's health, and your baby's gestational age.

Breech or Transverse Presentation

Breech and transverse presentations are fairly rare. Breech presentation (feet, legs, or buttocks over the cervix) happens in 3 to 4 percent of pregnancies. Transverse presentation (one shoulder over the cervix) happens in less than 1 percent of pregnancies.

If a baby is breech or transverse at thirty-six weeks gestation, most caregivers will advise a planned cesarean. Here's why: A baby lying transverse at this point cannot be born vaginally and usually won't turn vertex (head over the cervix) before labor begins. A breech baby can be born vaginally, and most vaginal breech births end with healthy babies and mothers. However, vaginal breech birth requires a specific set of skills that many caregivers haven't developed. Also, vaginal breech birth raises the risk of umbilical cord prolapse (cord-first birth), cord compression, difficulty delivering the head, and spinal injury. Many caregivers prefer the risks of a cesarean over the risks of a vaginal breech birth.

A breech baby may turn vertex with help from the mother and/or caregiver. If your baby is breech and you want to try to avoid a cesarean, the methods described in the following paragraphs may be helpful.

External Version

External version is a procedure performed by your caregiver. Your caregiver manipulates the outside of your belly to try to turn your baby vertex. This procedure works best between thirty-six and thirty-eight weeks gestation.

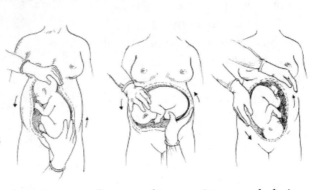

Before a version, your caregiver does an ultrasound to monitor your baby's heart rate; to determine the positions of your baby, the placenta, and the

Notes:

umbilical cord; to assess the amount of amniotic fluid; to examine your uterus; and to plan which way to turn your baby. If your fluid is low, if your placenta is anterior (implanted on the front of your uterus), or if your uterus is abnormal in any way, your caregiver may decide not to perform the version.

If your caregiver decides to go ahead with the version, he or she may first give you an injection of a tocolytic medication. This medication relaxes your uterus. Then, using ultrasound for guidance and to continue monitoring your baby's heart rate, your caregiver places his or her hands on your belly and carefully pushes or lifts your baby. These motions encourage your baby to roll forward or backward. A version usually takes five to ten minutes to complete.

The pressure of a version may be uncomfortable or even painful for you. To reduce your discomfort and facilitate the process, breathe rhythmically and try to relax your abdomen.

If your baby's heart rate indicates distress at any point, your caregiver stops the procedure immediately. If your water breaks or if labor contractions begin, you may need medical care. If your placenta starts detaching during a version or if your baby's heart rate indicates distress after your caregiver halts the procedure, you may need an emergency cesarean. For these reasons, your caregiver will probably perform a version at a hospital.

About 65 percent of external versions succeed. Failed versions are those in which the baby either doesn't turn at all or turns vertex only to flip back to breech. After a failed version, your caregiver may try again. But after most failed versions, the babies are born by cesarean.

Acupuncture

Acupuncture may help turn a breech baby. Several scientific studies and reviews of the research suggest that the success rate of acupuncture—including the related practice of moxibustion—in turning breech babies is at least 50 percent.

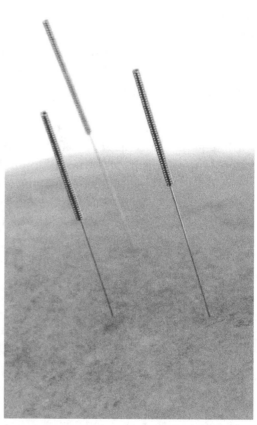

To encourage a breech baby to turn vertex, a trained acupuncturist inserts fine needles through the skin at two specific points. These points, both called Urinary Bladder 67, lie on the outside tips of the little toes.

The practitioner may also perform moxibustion at these points. Moxibustion is the placement of burning herbs close to the acupuncture points. An acupuncturist can teach you how to do moxibustion so you can repeat the practice multiple times per day.

Common Labor Interventions

Certain labor interventions are common for women laboring in North America. These interventions include IV catheters, electronic fetal monitoring, labor induction, medications, episiotomy, delivery by forceps or vacuum extractor, and cesarean section.

IV Catheters

Some hospitals routinely insert IV catheters into all women in labor. Other hospitals insert IV catheters only if needed, such as to give Pitocin, antibiotics, pain medications, or fluids. An IV catheter poses some mild risks, and it limits your mobility because you're attached to a wheeled pole and bag of fluids. Ask your caregiver whether IV catheters are routine at your birthplace. If so, ask if you can have a saline lock instead. A saline lock requires inserting an IV catheter, but doesn't involve hooking it to the IV bag and pole until fluids are needed.

Electronic Fetal Monitoring

In most labors, a caregiver monitors the baby's heart rate. The baby's heart rate is an important indicator of his or her well-being.

Normally, the fetal heart beats 120 to 160 times per minute. The fetal heart rate (FHR) varies within this normal range. FHR variations occur in response to factors such as the baby's movement, the mother's position or temperature, medications given to the mother, and uterine contractions.

If a baby is not coping well with labor due to prematurity or a health problem, his or her heart rate may become less variable or may vary outside the normal range. This condition is called fetal distress. A baby in distress requires close monitoring. He or she might also need medical help.

Your caregiver can monitor your baby's heart rate using two methods. These methods are auscultation and electronic fetal monitoring (EFM).

Auscultation is listening to your baby's heart rate intermittently before a contraction, during a contraction, and after a contraction. Your caregiver can perform auscultation using either a fetoscope (a type of stethoscope) or a Doptone (a handheld device that converts ultrasound readings of your baby's heartbeat into sounds).

Electronic fetal monitoring is the use of two electronic sensors to detect contractions and fetal heart rate. Your caregiver can perform EFM intermittently or continuously, using external or internal sensors. EFM records its readings electronically. It may also produce a printout or transmit readings to a video screen.

- With **external EFM**, your caregiver wraps two belts around your abdomen. One belt carries a Doptone to read your baby's heart rate. The other belt carries a sensor to read changes in uterine muscle tone.
- With **internal EFM**, your caregiver attaches an electrode to your baby's scalp to read fetal heart rate. To detect contractions, your caregiver may use either an external belt or a catheter inserted into your uterus. Internal EFM is possible only after your water has broken. Caregivers typically use this method only when external EFM isn't working well.

Most hospital-based caregivers prefer continuous EFM because it saves staff time. However, continuous EFM usually prevents a woman from moving around freely during labor, which may affect labor progress and her ability to stay comfortable.

Notes:

Continuous EFM may also be associated with increased cesarean birth (see page 82) and instrument delivery (see page 81). If you value freedom of movement in labor, you may prefer auscultation or a wireless type of EFM called telemetry. If you or your baby has health problems, if your pregnancy is high risk, or if your labor is complicated, your caregiver will probably use continuous EFM.

Labor Induction

Labor induction is attempting to start labor before it starts on its own. However, unless there's a medical reason, it's strongly recommended that labor isn't induced before the thirty-ninth week of pregnancy.[7] The following paragraphs describe common medical and nonmedical reasons and techniques for inducing labor. You'll also learn about the benefits and risks of labor induction.

Reasons for Induction

In the following list, items one through five are medical indications (health-related reasons supported by scientific evidence) for inducing labor. Items six through nine are nonmedical reasons for induction.

1. **Prolonged pregnancy:** Some caregivers consider a pregnancy to be prolonged at various points between forty and forty-two weeks. A pregnancy is officially prolonged (also called postterm or postdate) when it continues past forty-two weeks. After forty-two weeks, a pregnancy has a 5 to 10 percent risk of postmaturity. In a postmature pregnancy, the baby's growth slows down or stops, the placenta functions poorly, and the risk of fetal death rises. If a caregiver determines via testing that your pregnancy is postmature, he or she will probably advise labor induction.

2. **Rupture of amniotic sac:** After your water breaks, you have a higher risk of infection. If labor doesn't start on its own within twenty-four hours, your caregiver may advise labor induction. If you have tested positive for GBS earlier in your pregnancy, your caregiver may recommend induction sooner.

3. **Intrauterine growth restriction (IUGR):** If your baby has IUGR (has stopped growing and thriving inside your body), your caregiver will probably advise labor induction. Even if your baby is premature, birth—as well as the following medical observation and treatment—will likely give your baby a better chance at good health than if you continue the pregnancy.

4. **Genital herpes:** A baby may catch herpes from his or her mother during a vaginal birth while active herpes sores are present. Herpes infection in a newborn can cause serious—and sometimes fatal—health problems. Herpes in a pregnant woman is most dangerous to her baby when the mother first catches the infection. A mother who contracts herpes in the third trimester should not birth her baby vaginally during an outbreak of sores. If you have genital herpes and are experiencing outbreaks in the third trimester, your caregiver may advise labor induction between outbreaks both to protect your baby and to prevent a cesarean. (See pages 82 and 84 for more information.)

5. **Maternal illness:** For PIH and some other illnesses in the mother, delivery of the baby is the only cure.

6. **Concern about a too-large baby (macrosomia):** If you have an ultrasound in your third trimester, your caregiver may note that your baby is growing fast or is large. If your baby appears large in comparison to your build, your caregiver may worry that if your baby grows any larger, he or she will be too large to fit through your pelvis during a vaginal birth. Your caregiver may advise labor induction to avoid such a situation. Although this

course of action seems reasonable, macrosomia is *not* a valid medical reason for induction. Here's why: Ultrasound does not provide precise measurements. It can only estimate a baby's size, and its margin of error is at least 10 percent. That means an ultrasound scan suggesting a very large baby has a good chance of being wrong. In addition, research shows that compared to letting labor start on its own, inducing labor for macrosomia is more likely to result in a stalled labor—and a subsequent cesarean. Finally, a baby's size is not a good predictor of delivery problems. Among babies who actually do get stuck in their mothers' pelvises, 70 percent weigh less than 8½ pounds (3.9 kg); they are of small or average size.

7. **Convenience:** A caregiver may recommend—or a mother may request—labor induction for convenience. Most caregivers belong to group practices. Caregivers attend births according to the group's rotating on-call schedule. If a caregiver is not on call when his or her client goes into labor, another caregiver attends the birth. A caregiver may prefer to induce labor for his or her clients so he or she can attend their births. Likewise, a mother may prefer induction so her caregiver can attend her birth. Or a mother may have other reasons to request an induction. For example, she may have a history of quick labor, may live far from her birthplace, or may have postpartum support available only within a certain window of time.

8. **Discomfort:** If you are very uncomfortable at the end of your pregnancy—for example, if you can't sleep, if the weather is very hot, if you have hemorrhoids or other aches and pains—you may be anxious to give birth. Labor induction may be very appealing to you.

9. **Term:** Some caregivers and mothers feel comfortable inducing labor anytime after thirty-nine weeks. However, it's important to remember that during the last few weeks of pregnancy, the baby's brain and other vital organs are still rapidly developing.[8]

Contraindications for Induction

Contraindications are conditions that make a medical treatment unsafe. If you have any of the following conditions, you should not undergo labor induction.
• transverse presentation of baby
• placenta previa
• outbreak of newly contracted genital herpes
• history of uterine fibroid surgery

Ways to Induce Labor

If you and your caregiver agree on labor induction, you have many possible methods at your disposal. In the following list, items one through eight are nonmedical ways to induce labor. Items nine through thirteen are medical induction methods. Before using or consenting to any method, discuss it with your caregiver.

1. **Sex:** This method is safe to try if your water hasn't broken yet. Orgasm makes your body release hormones called oxytocin and prostaglandins. Both hormones can cause your uterus to contract and help start labor. In addition, semen contains prostaglandins.

2. **Nipple stimulation:** This method makes your body release oxytocin. You can stimulate your nipples by lightly stroking them, by having your partner do so, or by using a breast pump. The contractions can become long and painful very quickly. Most caregivers prefer that a woman be at her birthplace before starting nipple stimulation.

Notes:

3. **Castor oil:** Castor oil makes your intestines contract, which in turn makes your body release prostaglandins. Most caregivers do not recommend castor oil because of its bad taste and because it carries the risk of painful diarrhea and dehydration.

4. **Walking:** A long walk may help start labor. Do not walk so fast that you cannot carry on a conversation. Do not get overheated.

5. **Acupressure:** Pressure on either the Hoku or the Spleen 6 acupressure points can cause uterine contractions. (See page 51 for more information on how to use acupressure on these points.)

6. **Acupuncture:** A trained professional can insert acupuncture needles or practice moxibustion (see page 72) at the Hoku and Spleen 6 points to encourage oxytocin and prostaglandin release.[9]

7. **Herbs:** Certain herbs, such as blue cohosh, black cohosh, evening primrose oil, black haw, and red raspberry leaves, can stimulate uterine contractions.[10] You can ingest such herbs in tea or tincture form. A tincture is a solution of herbal extract in alcohol. Herbs, like all medicines, have side effects. Use them only with help from a trained professional.

8. **Homeopathy:** Homeopathy is a type of medical care that treats a disease or condition by administering tiny doses of a remedy that would produce symptoms of the disease or condition in a healthy person. Its goal is to stimulate the body's ability to heal itself. Homeopathic remedies are extracts of natural substances highly diluted in alcohol or water. Because the remedies are so diluted, they are generally safe. However, it's best to use homeopathy with help from a trained professional.

9. **Dilator:** Your caregiver may advise using a dilator to put pressure on the inside of your cervix, which encourages your cervix to ripen (soften), efface (thin or shorten), and dilate (open). Two types of dilators are available. A balloon dilator is a rubber balloon on the end of a catheter. Your caregiver inserts the balloon inside your cervix and inflates it with a saline (salt water) solution. A hygroscopic dilator is a device made of absorbent, moisture-sensitive material such as laminaria (dried, sterilized seaweed) or Lamicel (a synthetic foam that works like laminaria). This dilator absorbs fluid from the cervix and vagina. The moisture makes the dilator expand.

10. **Membrane sweeping:** Sweeping (sometimes called stripping) of the membranes is a procedure performed by your caregiver. Your caregiver inserts a finger through your cervix and sweeps in a circular motion to detach the lower part of your amniotic sac from the inside of your uterus. This procedure stimulates prostaglandin release and also mechanically dilates the cervix. Research shows that membrane sweeping alone usually does not induce labor. Sweeping is, however, helpful when used along with other methods. It can reduce the amount of Pitocin needed, may help speed up labor, and may help prevent a cesarean.[11] Drawbacks include moderate pain, cramping, and mild bleeding.

11. **Amniotomy:** Amniotomy is artificially rupturing your amniotic sac. This procedure is also called artificial rupture of membranes (AROM). To perform AROM, your caregiver inserts an amniohook (a device that looks like a large crochet hook) through your cervix and into your uterus.

amniotomy

Your caregiver uses the amniohook to break your water. This procedure is thought to stimulate prostaglandin release and put pressure on the cervix. Research shows that AROM alone usually does not induce labor. AROM can, however, be helpful in speeding up labor. Drawbacks include increased risk of umbilical cord prolapse or compression, infection, bleeding, fetal injury, and emergency cesarean.[12]

12. **Prostaglandin medication:** If you and your caregiver have agreed on labor induction, but your cervix is not ripe, your caregiver may administer a synthetic prostaglandin. This is a medication that mimics your own hormones to help ripen your cervix so it can efface and dilate. Synthetic prostaglandin is available in two forms: a gel called dinoprostone placed next to your cervix either directly or via a tampon-like device, or a pill or capsule containing misoprostol either taken orally or placed in your vagina. Research shows that both forms of prostaglandin medication are effective at ripening the cervix and that they may also stimulate contractions. Drawbacks include limited mobility after vaginal administration, increased risk of nausea, vomiting, diarrhea, infection, and fever. In addition, synthetic prostaglandins can overstimulate the uterus. Your caregiver must carefully follow dosage and timing guidelines to prevent severe contractions, fetal distress, and rupture of the uterus.[13]

13. **Pitocin:** Pitocin is a widely used brand of synthetic oxytocin. Syntocinon is another brand. Both forms of synthetic oxytocin mimic your body's natural oxytocin to help start uterine contractions. Your caregiver administers Pitocin directly into your bloodstream through an IV. Research shows that Pitocin is effective in starting or speeding up labor when the cervix is already ripe. Drawbacks include immobility due to IV lines and continuous EFM, restrictions on eating and drinking, contractions that are more painful than natural ones, and increased risk of cesarean.

Risks of Labor Induction

Labor induction may benefit you physically and/or mentally for the reasons described on pages 74–75. Be sure to weigh these benefits against the drawbacks of the specific method you use (see pages 75–77), as well as the following general risks of induction.

Your baby develops and matures right up to the moment that labor starts on its own. If you induce labor, you may increase your baby's risk of problems related to prematurity, such as difficulty breathing and feeding, impaired hearing and vision, jaundice (see page 111), and vulnerability to infection.

• Medical induction methods often begin a cascade of medical interventions, such as IV fluids, continuous EFM, restricted eating and drinking, and confinement to bed. These interventions can make your labor more challenging to cope with and can introduce complications.

• Induced labor often seems longer than spontaneous labor because the mother is focused on labor progress from before the first contraction.

• All labor induction methods carry health risks. The most common ones are uterine hyperstimulation (dangerously severe contractions) and fetal distress.

• Induced labor contractions tend to be more painful than natural ones.

• Labor induction doesn't always work. Failed inductions often result in cesareans.

Pain Relief Medications

Your options for coping with labor pain depend partly on your birthplace. If you have your baby at a birth center or at home, you'll be able to use most or all of the labor coping methods discussed in Chapter 4.

If you give birth in a hospital, the facility's policies, staff, and equipment may hinder you from using many non-drug coping methods. Pain medication may be one of just a few options. If you want to use non-drug coping methods, and medical necessity doesn't rule them out, you should challenge policies, staff, and situations that hinder you. Non-drug methods have no negative side effects on a healthy mother and baby experiencing a normal birth. By contrast, no one can know in advance how a drug will affect an individual mother, baby, or labor.

Regardless of your birthplace or your pain-relief preferences, it's a good idea to learn about all labor comfort measures. Your labor may not go as you expect, rendering your preferences unnecessary or impossible. For example, if you are planning an unmedicated birth, unforeseen challenges or complications may necessitate medications. If you're planning to use medications, they may not work well for you. Or your labor may progress rapidly, leaving no time for medications.

The following paragraphs describe the primary pain relief medication methods available in most North American hospitals. You'll learn how each method works, how it may benefit you, and what drawbacks it presents to you and your baby.

Epidural Catheter and Spinal Block

The epidural catheter and the spinal block are two related methods of delivering medication into your lower back, near nerve roots in your spine. Here's how each method works:

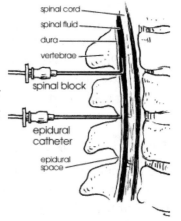

- For an **epidural catheter**, an anesthesiologist or nurse anesthetist inserts a needle into the epidural space in your spine. This is the space inside your vertebrae between the bone and the dura (the membrane surrounding your spinal cord). The caregiver threads a catheter (thin plastic tube) through the needle, removes the needle, tapes the catheter to your back, and attaches the catheter to a device that steadily releases small amounts of medication. Medication given by epidural takes effect within minutes, and pain relief lasts as long as medication continues to flow through the catheter.
- For a **spinal block**, a caregiver gives you a single injection of medication by inserting a needle into the intrathecal space. This is the space inside the dura where cerebrospinal fluid flows, between the dura and the spinal cord. A spinal block takes effect within minutes and may last up to a few hours.

The medication delivered via epidural catheter or spinal block is usually a combination of an anesthetic (a drug that blocks nerves from sending pain impulses to your brain) and an analgesic (a drug that acts on your brain so you don't recognize pain impulses). The medication does not affect your mental state. When injected into your spine, the medication affects the region of your body served by the nerve roots in the injection area. The region may be as small as your lower back and abdomen or as large as the area from your toes to your chest. Lower doses of medication numb the region while allowing some muscle control. Higher doses of medication both numb the region and temporarily suppress muscle control.

When you can receive an epidural catheter or a spinal block depends on your caregiver. Some caregivers, concerned about the risk of slowing or stalling labor, prefer that a woman be in active labor before receiving this type of anesthesia. Most experts agree that it's best to wait until the cervix is at least 4 or 5 centimeters dilated. Other caregivers permit epidural or spinal anesthesia any time during labor.

Epidural and spinal anesthesia release a small amount of medication into a limited area of the body. Little or no medication reaches the baby. For most women, this type of anesthesia provides good pain relief.

This type of pain relief does have drawbacks, however. Possible side effects for you include itching, nausea, fever, low blood pressure, sedation, and difficulty emptying your bladder or bowels. You may not feel the urge to push your baby out, which can lengthen or complicate the pushing stage. These side effects can lead to medical interventions, such as administering the drug Pitocin to kick-start labor (see page 77), episiotomy (see page 80), the use of forceps or a vacuum extractor to pull your baby out of the birth canal (see page 81), or cesarean birth if your baby does not descend far enough into the vagina. Secondary side effects that may result from interventions include uterine hyperstimulation (contractions that are too long, strong, or frequent), variations in baby's heart rate, and serious tearing of the perineum (the tissue between your vagina and anus).[14]

To maintain safety and minimize side effects, caregivers must take various precautions and perform certain interventions alongside epidural or spinal anesthesia. If you have this type of pain relief, you'll be confined to bed. Your eating and drinking will likely be restricted. You will have IV fluids, a bladder catheter, and continuous electronic monitoring of blood pressure, contractions, and your baby's heart rate. You may find the lack of mobility, the inability to eat or drink, and the transformation of your birth into a medical event frustrating or fatiguing.

Women who have epidural or spinal anesthesia in labor also face postpartum side effects. Their babies may receive a small amount of the medication, which can alter normal newborn behavior. In addition, their babies have a higher risk of jaundice. (See page 111.) A woman who has had epidural or spinal anesthesia may have a headache, a backache, or pain at the injection site for days or weeks. Compared to women who have unmedicated births, women who have an epidural catheter or spinal block are less likely to initiate breastfeeding, more likely to stop breastfeeding sooner, and more likely to have breastfeeding challenges. This side effect increases a variety of health risks for both mother and baby.[15]

If you've had epidural or spinal anesthesia and your labor is progressing normally, delayed pushing is a good strategy. You may not feel the urge to push, but your uterus continues to squeeze your baby out on its own. Delayed pushing is letting your uterus do this work—while you rest and avoid pushing—until your baby crowns or until you feel an urge to push. This method is also called laboring down. By laboring down, you can avoid exhausting yourself and stressing your baby. You can also reduce your risk of tearing or needing an instrument delivery (see page 81) or a cesarean (see page 82).

If you use delayed pushing, tell your caregiver when you feel a pushing urge. If you don't feel an urge, your caregiver will tell you when your baby is crowning. When it's time to push, you can use directed pushing (see page 59).

Notes:

Narcotics

Narcotics (or narcotic-like drugs) are systemic analgesics. They are delivered intravenously or by injection into a muscle. They act on receptors in your brain so you don't recognize pain impulses. Laboring mothers who use narcotics typically feel the peak of

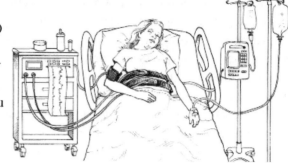

each contraction, but not the beginning or the end of it. This pain relief method usually takes effect within ten minutes and lasts sixty to ninety minutes. Most caregivers prefer to administer narcotics when birth is two or more hours away. That is, they will typically give narcotics in early or active labor, but not in transition or during pushing. This timing lets the medication wear off before birth.

Most laboring women who receive IV narcotics report significant pain relief. This method works well for women who are coping well with the pain at the peak of each contraction but need a longer break to rest between contractions. Compared to an epidural catheter or spinal block, narcotics are quick and easy to administer. And unlike epidural or spinal anesthesia, narcotics don't interfere directly with labor progress or the ability to push.

However, narcotics do have some drawbacks. They don't provide complete pain relief. They don't work well if you're having trouble coping with the peak of each contraction. You may have to have IV fluids and continuous electronic fetal monitoring. You may also be confined to bed. In addition, narcotics have several mental and physical side effects. Because you receive these drugs via your bloodstream, they affect your entire body. Possible side effects for you include sleepiness, lethargy, nausea, vomiting, itching, dizziness, confusion, respiratory depression, and oxygen deficiency. Possible side effects for your baby include variations in heart rate, slow breathing, poor muscle tone, and increased risk of addictive behavior in later life. A possible side effect for both you and your baby is difficulty breastfeeding.[16]

Antinausea Medication

Nausea and vomiting are common side effects of epidural, spinal, and narcotic pain relief. As a result, many caregivers administer an antinausea medication along with the pain medication. Antinausea medication works well for some women. But for others, it has little or no effect. Caregivers do not usually prescribe antinausea drugs for women in unmedicated labor who begin vomiting in the transition phase. Vomiting is a common sign of transition, and it's typically short-lived.

Episiotomy

An episiotomy is a surgical incision to enlarge your vaginal opening. If you have not had epidural or spinal anesthesia, your caregiver first administers a perineal block to numb your perineum. Then your caregiver makes a small incision in your perineum, from the rear part of your vagina toward your anus.

Your caregiver may recommend an episiotomy if your pushing stage is prolonged. Research shows that episiotomy can shorten the second stage of labor five to fifteen minutes. An episiotomy may be necessary if your baby is in distress, if your caregiver suspects that your baby is having trouble moving through your pelvis, or if you're exhausted or otherwise unable to push effectively. In addition, your caregiver may perform an episiotomy if he or she plans to use instruments to help deliver your baby. (See the next section for more information on instrument delivery.)

If you have an episiotomy, your caregiver repairs it after your baby's birth. During the recovery stage, your caregiver stitches shut the incision to help it heal.

Routine episiotomy is neither necessary nor recommended. A recent review of the research found that routine episiotomy is harmful to women. It increases a woman's pain and healing time. It also raises the risk of serious tearing, bladder and bowel incontinence (leaking urine, feces, or gas), and pain during sexual intercourse.[17]

Instrument Delivery

If you have not had epidural or spinal anesthesia, your caregiver may give you a perineal block before performing an instrument delivery. Instrument delivery is using a vacuum extractor or forceps to help your baby exit your body. Your caregiver may also perform an episiotomy (see previous section).

A vacuum extractor is a silicone suction cup at the end of a long handle. To use it, your caregiver attaches the suction cup to the top of your baby's head.

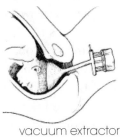

vacuum extractor

Forceps are long steel tongs. The paddles of the tongs are curved to fit the shape of a baby's head. To use forceps, your caregiver inserts the paddles into your vagina one at a time. Your caregiver positions the paddles snugly around your baby's head.

While you push, your caregiver pulls carefully on the handle of the vacuum extractor or forceps. Once your baby's head emerges from your vagina, your caregiver detaches the vacuum extractor or forceps. You push out the rest of your baby's body on your own.

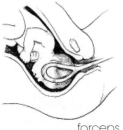

forceps

For instrument delivery, caregivers tend to use the instrument they trained with in medical school. Some caregivers are proficient with both vacuum extractors and forceps.

Your caregiver may recommend instrument delivery if your pushing stage is prolonged, if your baby is in distress, if your caregiver suspects that your baby is having trouble moving through your pelvis, or if you're exhausted or otherwise unable to push effectively. Women who have received epidural or spinal anesthesia are more likely to experience instrument delivery than women who haven't. If the instruments don't help, your caregiver stops using them and will probably recommend a cesarean.

Research shows that instrument delivery is safe when caregivers follow professional guidelines for the use of vacuum extractors and forceps. However, babies commonly suffer scrapes, bruises, and swelling on their heads or faces from these instruments. They also face a higher risk of jaundice. (See page 111.) Drawbacks for mothers include perineal injury and pain—either from use of the instruments or from prior episiotomy.[18]

Cesarean Birth

A cesarean birth is a type of surgery. In this surgery, a caregiver cuts incisions in a pregnant woman's abdomen and uterus and lifts the baby out by hand.

The following paragraphs describe common reasons for cesarean birth. You'll also learn what happens before, during, and after the surgery and about the benefits and risks of cesarean birth.

Reasons for Cesarean Birth

In the following situations, most caregivers agree that the benefits of a cesarean outweigh its risks. These are clear medical indications for cesarean birth.

- **Severe preeclampsia:** See page 70 for more information.
- **Placental abruption:** See page 70.
- **Placenta previa:** See page 70.
- **Umbilical cord prolapse:** Cord-first birth.
- **Transverse presentation of baby:** See page 71.
- **Cervical tumor:** A tumor on or near the cervix blocks the baby's exit from the uterus.
- **Injured or deformed pelvis:** If a mother's pelvic bones are deformed or injured, she may be able to carry a baby safely but not give birth vaginally.
- **Genital herpes contracted during the third trimester:** Herpes in a pregnant woman is most dangerous to the baby when the mother first catches the infection. If this occurs at the end of pregnancy, cesarean surgery is one of two safe ways to deliver the baby. (See pages 74 and 84 for more information.)
- **Maternal human immunodeficiency virus (HIV):** One of the main ways children become infected with HIV is mother-to-child transmission during labor and birth. If a blood test indicates that you have advanced HIV or that your HIV is not well-controlled with medications, cesarean is the safest way to birth your baby.[19]
- **Triplets or more, or twins when the first baby's presentation is breech or transverse:** If you're carrying multiple babies, your uterus may be overstretched and unable to contract efficiently. In addition, crowded conditions inside the uterus make it difficult for multiples to get into good positions for vaginal birth. Triplets and higher-order multiples are rarely born vaginally for these reasons. Twins can be born vaginally if the first baby is vertex, but if it isn't, a cesarean is usually necessary.
- **Uterine rupture:** Uterine rupture is when the uterus tears open during labor. The most common sign of uterine rupture is sudden, severe fetal distress. Without immediate surgery, uterine rupture can be fatal for the mother and/or the baby. When uterine rupture occurs, the caregiver performs an emergency cesarean. If the uterus is severely damaged, the caregiver may also perform a hysterectomy (surgical removal of the uterus). Uterine rupture is rare, but its risk increases in certain circumstances. For example, a woman is at higher risk for uterine rupture if she has had a cesarean with a high vertical uterine incision, has had three or more cesareans with low horizontal incisions, has had surgery to remove large uterine fibroid tumors, has had five or more full-term pregnancies, is carrying multiples or a transverse baby, or is receiving labor-inducing medication.[20]

- **Other serious health problems in the baby or mother:** Some birth defects, diseases, and other health problems make vaginal birth more risky than cesarean.

In the situations described in the following list, some caregivers recommend a cesarean while others do not. These are debatable medical reasons or nonmedical reasons for cesarean.

- **Failure to progress in labor:** Failure to progress means that either dilation or pushing is taking longer than expected. It is the most common reason North American caregivers recommend a cesarean. Sometimes caregivers call failure to progress "cephalo-pelvic disproportion" (CPD). CPD means that the caregiver thinks the baby's head is too big to exit the mother's pelvis. However, CPD is impossible to predict or diagnose. And a long labor or birth isn't intrinsically dangerous. If mother and baby are holding up well, failure to progress is not a clear medical indication for cesarean. Alternatives to cesarean are measures that get labor moving or facilitate birth. These include movement and position changes, speeding up contractions with labor induction methods, using coping methods or pain medication to help the mother relax, warm compresses to help the perineum stretch, and instrument delivery. If these measures don't work, if the baby isn't doing well, or if the mother becomes exhausted, a cesarean may be necessary.

- **Fetal heart rate variations suggesting fetal distress:** This is the second most common reason caregivers recommend a cesarean. Monitoring a baby's heart rate is easy. But interpreting a baby's heart rate is tricky. Different caregivers may interpret the same readings in different ways. A change such as slowing of the baby's heart rate may occur because a baby isn't coping well with labor. But it may also occur because a baby *is* coping well. There's no way to know for sure what an FHR reading means. This is why FHR variation alone is not a clear medical indication for cesarean. One alternative to cesarean in this case is waiting to see whether the FHR pattern improves or stays stable. Another alternative is assessing the baby's well-being via fetal scalp stimulation. To perform fetal scalp stimulation, the caregiver presses on the baby's scalp. If the FHR accelerates, it's a sign that baby is doing well. If the FHR shows no change, it's a sign that baby may be in distress. If FHR remains worrisome after a wait-and-see period and/or fetal scalp stimulation, a cesarean may be necessary.

- **History of previous cesarean:** This is the third most common reason caregivers recommend a cesarean. Many caregivers recommend repeat cesareans because they are concerned about the risk of uterine rupture in a vaginal birth after cesarean (VBAC). (See page 82 for more information on uterine rupture.) Scientific evidence, however, does not clearly indicate that cesarean is the best choice for all women with prior cesareans. The benefits and risks of VBAC versus cesarean depend on the details of each case, such as how many prior cesareans a woman has had, how long ago the last one occurred, what kind of uterine scar she has, whether infection occurred after a prior cesarean, and whether labor is induced for VBAC. The overall risk of uterine rupture is 325 in 100,000 during a VBAC and 26 in 100,000 during a planned repeat cesarean. The overall risk of fetal death is 130 in 100,000 during a VBAC and 50 in 100,000 during a repeat cesarean. The overall risk of maternal death is less than 4 in 100,000 during a VBAC and more than 13 in 100,000 during a repeat cesarean.[21]

- **Genital herpes recurrence with active sores at the beginning of labor:** In such cases, some caregivers recommend a cesarean. Others don't, because cesarean itself carries risks (see page 88) and doesn't guarantee the baby protection from herpes. In addition, the rate of transmission during vaginal birth is low when the mother has had herpes since early pregnancy or since before pregnancy. Over time, the mother develops antibodies to fight the virus, and she passes these antibodies along to her baby.[22]
- **Breech presentation of baby:** See page 71.
- **Twins or more, regardless of presentation:** See also page 82.
- **Macrosomia:** See page 74.
- **Pelvic floor preservation:** Some women and caregivers believe that cesarean can help preserve the pelvic floor (the muscles between the pubic bone and the tailbone) by avoiding stretching, cuts, or tearing—thus preventing incontinence and sexual problems. But research shows that this belief is mistaken. By six months postpartum, the rates of incontinence and sexual problems are the same in women who birthed vaginally and women who had cesareans. The most effective way to preserve the pelvic floor during labor and birth is to avoid, if possible, interventions such as continuous EFM (see page 73), epidural and spinal anesthesia (see page 78), lying on the back, pressing on the uterus during pushing, directed pushing (see page 59), episiotomy (see page 80), and instrument delivery (see page 81). Other ways to preserve the pelvic floor are maintaining a healthy weight, not smoking, and exercising the pelvic floor muscles (see page 11).[23]
- **Fear, convenience, and other nonmedical reasons:** Some women request cesarean birth to avoid labor pain, to feel more control over the process of birth, to schedule birth for a convenient time, or to cope with fear of vaginal birth. Cesareans performed for such reasons are called elective cesareans. Professional organizations for ob-gyns in North America take varied stances on whether an ob-gyn may ethically perform an elective cesarean. Scientific research, however, shows that cesarean surgery without a clear medical reason is not advisable unless the woman's concerns about vaginal birth can't be resolved in other ways, and cesarean is the only way to protect her mental health. (See page 88 for more information on the risks of cesarean birth.)

Preparing for Cesarean

You may be planning a cesarean birth out of necessity. Or you may find yourself undergoing an unexpected cesarean. You can take certain steps during pregnancy to ensure the best possible cesarean birth—planned or unplanned, wanted or unwanted. Following are some ideas that can help you have a safe and satisfying cesarean birth.

- **Care for your body during pregnancy:** Eat well, exercise regularly if possible, and get adequate rest. The healthier you are before surgery, the quicker you'll recover from it.
- **Get educated:** Read books, take a class, and discuss the procedure with your caregiver. Understand the various reasons for cesarean. Learn about evidence-based cesarean practices. Know the policies regarding cesarean surgery at your birthplace. Tour the birthplace, including the special care nursery.

- **Seek and develop a good caregiver-patient relationship:** If you have a caregiver you trust and work to develop a good relationship with him or her, you'll find it easier to obtain the information you need. And you're more likely to feel respected and properly cared for.
- **Participate in decision-making:** If you feel knowledgeable about cesarean and have a good relationship with your caregiver, you'll have the confidence to speak your mind. Joining the decision-making process can give you a sense of control over your birth. Discuss cesarean scenarios with your caregiver even if you expect to have a vaginal birth. Prepare a cesarean birth plan and work with your caregiver to implement it.
- **Plan for birth support:** If possible, arrange to have two support people—for example, your partner and a doula—present during your surgical prep, surgery, and recovery. If you and your baby need to be separated, one support person can be with you while the other is with your baby.
- **Plan for postpartum:** Take a breastfeeding class to prepare for the challenges of nursing after cesarean. Arrange for plenty of help for the first two weeks at home.
- **Wait as long as possible to have a planned cesarean:** Have your cesarean after labor starts if there's no urgent medical reason for doing it sooner. If you must schedule your surgery before labor begins, ask to have it as close as possible to your due date. This strategy can reduce your baby's risk of breathing problems and other complications of prematurity.
- **Insist on contact with your baby as soon and as much as possible:** Early, frequent mother–baby contact after cesarean can enhance bonding and minimize breastfeeding problems.
- **Control your pain:** Use enough pain medication to stay comfortable. If you're in constant pain, you'll find it difficult to move, bond with and care for your baby, and breastfeed.

What Happens

If you are having a planned cesarean, you can fill out the hospital paperwork in advance. You can also arrange to complete any necessary tests and lab work before the day of surgery.

At some point before your surgery, you stop eating and drinking. Your caregiver will provide specific instructions. General guidelines advise performing a cesarean at least two hours after the last drink of clear liquids, at least six hours after a light meal, and at least eight hours after a regular meal. Fasting ensures that your stomach is empty during surgery. Although most caregivers perform cesareans with epidural or spinal anesthesia, general anesthesia occasionally becomes necessary. Having an empty stomach reduces your risk of vomiting under general anesthesia and inhaling your stomach contents, which can lead to pneumonia.

Your caregiver will probably ask you to arrive at the hospital two hours before your surgery appointment. Upon arrival, you sign a form to certify that you understand why you're having a cesarean, that you understand the procedure's benefits and risks, and that you give your consent for the surgery.

A nurse helps prepare you for the cesarean. The nurse inserts an intravenous line, through which you receive medication and fluids. He or she positions EFM sensors as well as devices to monitor your blood pressure, oxygen levels, and heart rate during surgery. Your surgeon and anesthesiologist meet with you to evaluate your condition and go over the procedure with you.

If your surgeon thinks body hair will interfere with the closing of your incision after surgery, the nurse clips your hair at the incision site. The nurse may also insert a urinary catheter. This procedure is uncomfortable. To avoid discomfort, you can request catheter insertion after you've received anesthesia.

Next, the anesthesiologist administers anesthesia. Most women receive a spinal block or an epidural catheter for cesarean surgery. (See page 78 for more information.) General anesthesia, which renders a patient unconscious, is rare for cesareans. Caregivers typically use it only when women can't tolerate—or when anesthesiologists can't successfully place—epidural or spinal anesthesia, when unplanned cesareans occur at small hospitals with limited anesthesia services, and for emergency cesareans.

The medical staff for your cesarean includes an anesthesiologist, a surgeon, an assisting doctor or midwife, a surgical nurse, and a pediatric nurse to care for your baby. Others may be present, too, if you or your baby has a health problem requiring special care.

In the operating room, you lie on your back with your left hip slightly elevated. Your anesthesiologist stays near your head. He or she is responsible for monitoring your vital signs, tracking your fluid intake and output, and maintaining the proper level of anesthesia. If you feel nausea, discomfort, or pain, you should tell the anesthesiologist.

The surgical nurse washes your abdomen with antiseptic, drapes a sheet over your body, and positions a screen between your chest and abdomen. The screen keeps you from seeing the surgery—which many people find disturbing or nauseating—and from touching the surgical area, thereby contaminating it with germs.

To begin the cesarean, your surgeon first makes an incision through your abdominal wall (the skin, fat, and connective tissue lying over your abdominal muscles). This is usually a low transverse incision. A low transverse incision is a horizontal cut about 1 inch (2.5 cm) above your pubic bone and about 4 to 6 inches (10 to 15 cm) long. In rare situations, the surgeon may make a classical incision. A classical incision is a vertical cut between your pubic bone and your navel. The classical incision is reserved for emergency cesareans and situations in which a low transverse incision is not possible or advisable, such as transverse presentation or when the mother is obese.

Your surgeon manually separates your abdominal muscles. Then he or she cuts through your peritoneum (the tough membrane surrounding all your abdominal organs) to reach your uterus. Your surgeon will probably make a low transverse incision in your uterus. Under rare conditions, such as transverse presentation or placenta previa, your surgeon may make a low vertical or high vertical uterine incision.

The surgeon then stretches the uterine incision wide enough to accommodate your baby's head. He or she cauterizes (closes off by burning) cut blood vessels to prevent hemorrhage. If your water has not yet broken, the surgeon ruptures your amniotic sac and suctions out the fluid.

Finally, your surgeon and assisting caregiver work together to remove your baby from your uterus. One reaches in and gently lifts your baby's presenting part (head or buttocks) while the other presses on your uterus to help your baby emerge. You feel pushing and pulling, but no pain if your anesthesia is well managed.

After cesarean birth, your baby's immediate care is similar to that of a baby born vaginally. (See Chapter 8 for information on newborn care in early postpartum.) A few procedures will be different. For example, your baby will receive immediate care at a warming table or in the nursery instead of on your abdomen. Your baby may need airway suctioning if you experienced little or no labor, which helps squeeze out fluids. Babies born by cesarean are more likely to have breathing difficulties. Your baby may need oxygen, medication to help lung development, and close observation. Other treatments may be necessary if your baby is premature and/or has health problems.

As soon as possible, your partner, doula, or nurse should hold your baby close to your head so you can get acquainted. If the staff have training in the most progressive techniques, they can place your baby on your chest during post-birth assessments and procedures. Immediate skin-to-skin contact is optimal for all babies and mothers when circumstances permit. Meanwhile, your surgeon begins repairing your incisions.

You receive Pitocin to cause uterine contractions, which prevents hemorrhage. The surgeon extracts your placenta by hand. Then he or she stitches shut your uterine incision, closes up your abdomen, and repairs your abdominal incision with stitches or staples and surgical glue.

During or after the surgery, you may feel pain in your shoulders from air that has entered your abdomen. You may also feel queasy, anxious, or shaky. Slow breathing may help you cope with these discomforts. In addition, you can ask for warm fluids in your IV, warm blankets, or medication. If you need medication, request one(s) that doesn't make you sleepy, so you don't miss your baby's initial alert period right after the birth.[24]

Recovering from a Cesarean

After your surgery, you stay in the hospital for two to four days. The staff watches your vital signs, checks your lochia (see page 100), monitors your digestion, and cares for your incision.

During the first day of your hospital stay, you may continue to receive pain medication through your IV line. Whether your medication is patient-controlled or administered by staff, take enough to stay comfortable. Controlling your pain enables you to rest, move about, and care for your baby. If you experience unpleasant side effects, such as drowsiness, nausea, or itching, request a lower dose or a different kind of pain medication. During the second day of your hospital stay, you may switch to oral pain medication. You can lower your dosage, switch to over-the-counter medications, or stop taking pain medication whenever you feel ready to do so.

Throughout your hospital stay, the staff encourages you to move about. Physical activity helps your blood circulation, digestion, and breathing. You should start small and add more movement gradually. For example, your first day may include brief, simple efforts to roll onto your side, sit, stand, walk, cough, breathe deeply, and stretch your feet and ankles. Your second through fourth days might include the aforementioned activities plus knee bends while lying in bed, rolling your shoulders, and contracting your abdominal muscles. After you leave the hospital, you can continue gradually increasing simple physical activities. Follow your caregiver's instructions regarding stair climbing, heavy lifting, driving, and sexual intercourse.

You should be able to resume normal eating and drinking whenever you wish. Doing so improves your digestion, boosts your energy, and speeds your recovery.

The hospital staff teaches you how to clean, dry, and examine your incision daily. You can resume normal showering and bathing on the second day after your cesarean. Wear loose clothing over your belly. You may feel discomfort at your incision site for up to six weeks.

If your incision is healing well but you feel that your belly is sagging or your incision is pulling when you move, you can practice splinting. Splinting is supporting your incision by pressing gently on it with your hand, a towel, or a pillow.

Risks of Cesarean Birth

A cesarean may benefit you physically and/or mentally for the reasons described on pages 82-83. Be sure to weigh these benefits against the risks of cesarean surgery. The following effects are more likely with cesarean than with vaginal birth. The explanations in parentheses describe the added risk of each effect with cesarean birth over the risk of that effect with vaginal birth.[25]

- **Effects on mothers around the time of birth:**
  * Longer time in hospital (very high additional risk)
  * Negative feelings about birth (very high additional risk)
  * Less early contact with baby (very high additional risk)
  * Pain (high to very high additional risk)
  * Infection (high additional risk)
  * Psychological trauma (high additional risk for unplanned cesarean)
  * Emergency hysterectomy (moderate additional risk)
  * Readmission to hospital (moderate additional risk)
  * Blood clots and stroke (low additional risk)
  * Maternal death (very low to low additional risk)
- **Ongoing effect on mothers:**
  * Bowel obstruction in years after birth (moderate additional risk)
- **Effects on babies:**
  * Not breastfeeding (high to very high additional risk)
  * Accidental surgical cuts (high additional risk)
  * Asthma (high additional risk)
  * Respiratory problems (moderate to high additional risk for cesarean before 39 weeks)
- **Effects on future pregnancies and births:**
  * Unwanted infertility (high to very high additional risk)
  * Deciding not to have more children due to negative feelings about childbirth (high additional risk)
  * Placenta previa (moderate additional risk after one cesarean, high additional risk after multiple cesareans)
  * Ectopic pregnancy—embryo implanted outside uterus (moderate additional risk)
  * Placenta accreta—placenta growing into uterine muscle (moderate additional risk)
  * Placental abruption (moderate additional risk)
  * Uterine rupture (moderate additional risk)
  * Maternal death in future pregnancies (very low additional risk)
- **Effect on future babies:**
  * Death of baby (moderate additional risk)

Avoiding Unnecessary Cesarean

If you have made an informed choice to avoid an unnecessary cesarean, you can use the following tips to help you reach your goal.[26]

- Find a caregiver and birthplace with a low rate of medical interventions.
- Write a birth plan to clarify your preferences and goals. (See Chapter 6.)
- Discuss your preferences and goals with your caregiver. Seek the best possible patient-caregiver match.
- Arrange labor support from a knowledgeable person, such as a doula (see page 96) or an experienced friend or relative, for you and your partner.
- Learn about and practice nonmedical methods for coping with labor pain. (See pages 50–57.)
- If your caregiver proposes a non-emergency cesarean, use the B-R-A-I-N method (see page 22) to make an informed decision.
- Research and discuss with your caregiver the benefits and risks of VBAC. (See page 83.)
- If your baby is breech, try the methods on pages 71–72 to encourage him or her to turn vertex. If possible, find a caregiver skilled in vaginal breech birth.
- If you fear childbirth, seek counseling.
- If you're birthing in a hospital, delay admission until you are in active labor.
- Avoid inducing labor for nonmedical reasons. If your labor is slow, try various methods to speed it up. (See pages 75–76.)
- Avoid continuous EFM. (See page 73.)
- Avoid epidural or spinal anesthesia. (See page 78.)
- Avoid unnecessary medical interventions.

Postpartum Complications

Some mothers and babies develop conditions that complicate the postpartum period. Knowing a little about them can help you cope if you find yourself facing a challenging recovery.

Postpartum Hemorrhage

Postpartum hemorrhage is severe bleeding (losing more than 2 cups or 500 ml of blood) in the first twenty-four hours after birth. It is a relatively common complication. Postpartum hemorrhage happens in 20 percent of births.

Postpartum hemorrhage can happen for the following three reasons.

1. **Poor uterine muscle tone:** If your uterus doesn't contract properly after birth, the blood vessels that were attached to the placenta don't close off. They bleed freely into your uterus. To encourage uterine contractions, you can nurse your baby or stroke your nipples. You or your caregiver can massage your belly. Or your caregiver can give you Pitocin.

2. **Tearing:** Tearing of your perineum, vagina, or cervix during birth can also cause excess bleeding. To control such bleeding, your caregiver will stitch up the tears. He or she may also pack your vagina with sterile gauze.

3. **Retained placenta:** Occasionally a woman's uterus doesn't push out her placenta after birth. Sometimes part of the placenta emerges, but placental fragments remain in the uterus. Any amount of retained placenta interferes with postpartum uterine contractions and leads to excess bleeding. If you retain some or all of your placenta after birth, your caregiver will manually

Notes:

remove the placenta and then give you Pitocin and massage your uterus to stimulate contractions. You can help the process by breastfeeding and performing self-massage. If you have placenta accreta and the placenta will not detach, you may need a hysterectomy.

If you experience postpartum hemorrhage for any reason, you may feel symptoms of shock, such as pale skin, a rapid heartbeat, shaking, lightheadedness, sweating, and chills. You may need IV fluids and/or a blood transfusion.

Neonatal Illness or Death

Some babies are born with health problems or die around the time of birth. Neonatal illness and death are uncommon, and sometimes parents have advance warning to help them prepare. In other cases, serious problems are unexpected.

If your baby has serious health problems at birth, he or she may need special care in a neonatal intensive care unit (NICU). If your birthplace doesn't have a NICU, your caregiver may transfer him or her to a hospital that does have one. A NICU is a protected environment designed for close observation and specialized care of sick or premature babies. In the NICU, highly trained doctors and nurses watch over your baby's progress and treatment twenty-four hours per day. They use special equipment to monitor your baby's condition at all times. They educate and update you about your baby's condition and treatment. They also show you how to be a part of your baby's care by providing breast milk, skin-to-skin contact, and other vital contributions.

If your baby is ill or dies, your whole family will need extra support. You and your partner will likely feel a mixture of shock, anxiety, and sadness. You will need to lean on each other and keep the lines of communication open. If you have older children, you'll need help in caring for them. You'll likely also need help with transportation, meals, housework, and sharing news about your baby. A network of relatives, friends, coworkers, and/or community organizations can join forces to give you the support you need.

Hospital staff, too, can provide valuable support. For example, a hospital social worker can help you deal with emotional and financial challenges and connect you with helpful community resources. A hospital chaplain can offer you spiritual care.

Thinking through the possibility of neonatal problems can help you cope with them if they occur. During pregnancy, consider how you might want to handle decisions related to prematurity, illness, birth defects, birth trauma, stillbirth, or newborn death. For example, who might be willing to assemble a support network for you? If your baby dies before labor begins, do you want an induction? Do you want to be conscious for the birth? How would you like to say good-bye to your baby? What keepsakes would you like to obtain? Would you prefer to recover with other postpartum mothers or in a different part of the hospital? Do you want an autopsy?

If neonatal problems do arise, and you have thought through them already, you won't have to make difficult decisions in the throes of shock and grief. And if you discuss your preferences with your partner and caregiver in advance, you'll be more likely to receive the care you need and want.

Chapter 6
Preparing for Birth

This chapter will help you get ready for your baby's birth. Now that you've learned as much as you can about childbirth, you'll be well equipped to write a birth plan. The following pages guide you through that process. They also help you line up labor support and think through the logistics of going into labor.

Birth Plan

A birth plan is a brief verbal or written statement that describes your preferences for care during childbirth and early postpartum.

Why Write a Birth Plan?

A birth plan is key to having a satisfying birth experience. The process of creating a birth plan helps you think through your feelings and beliefs about birth and newborn care. It helps you discover and consider the options available to you. It encourages you to do the work of studying your options and deciding your preferences before labor starts. Finally, putting your preferences in writing increases your chances of receiving the care you desire.

A birth plan is also useful for those around you. It opens the lines of communication among you, your support person, and your caregiver. It helps you understand each other and either develop a stronger relationship or seek a better match. It provides a clear and easy way to convey your priorities and preferences to all staff and support people attending your birth.

Your Birth Plan

To write a birth plan, follow these steps:

1. **Educate yourself.** At least a few months before your due date, learn about the physical process of childbirth and the procedures commonly used by maternity caregivers. You can learn the basics of childbirth and maternity care in this book. You can also take a childbirth class and consult other books, websites, your caregiver, and experienced friends and relatives.
2. **Investigate your options.** Find out which maternity care options are available through your caregiver and birthplace. You can learn about your care options by talking with your caregiver or your caregiver's staff, by visiting the websites of your caregiver and birthplace, by taking a birth class sponsored by your caregiver or birthplace, or by taking a tour of your birthplace.
3. **Reflect and decide.** Examine your feelings and beliefs about birth and about different maternity care practices. Among the options available to you, decide which care practices you prefer in the various stages and scenarios of childbirth.
4. **Draft a birth plan.** Write a document outlining your maternity care preferences. You can use one of the worksheets in this chapter as a guide.
5. **Discuss and adjust.** When you are ready to discuss your birth plan with your caregiver, schedule a longer appointment so you'll have enough time for a thorough discussion. Share your birth plan with your caregiver. Compare priorities and beliefs. Reflect on your discussion. If necessary, adjust your preferences, negotiate or compromise with your caregiver, or seek a different caregiver or birthplace.
6. **Write a final birth plan.** Prepare a final birth plan summarizing your care preferences. Keep it concise. If possible, do not use a worksheet. Rather, write a personal statement addressing your care team. For each main topic, write a short paragraph or a bulleted list highlighting essential information. Use friendly, respectful language. Show that you understand the unpredictable nature of birth and that you realize unwanted procedures are sometimes medically necessary. Make copies of your birth plan for you, your partner, your caregiver, your birthplace, and your doula or other support person. Pack a copy or two in your birth bag as well.

Birth Plan Worksheets

Worksheet 1: No Medication, Minimal Intervention

Birth Plan	
We are excited to be working with (caregiver) and (birthplace) and their staff as we welcome our child into the world. We look forward to sharing this joyous occasion with you.	
Our goal is a totally natural birth. Our top priority is a healthy mother and baby.	
We appreciate all the support and encouragement you can provide toward these ends. We believe (father or partner)'s active participation, along with the care of our doula, (doula), will enable (mother) to achieve a natural birth.	
Assuming mom and baby are fine, these are our preferences:	
We prefer to experience a drug-free labor and birth.	We are fully aware of our options and request that the staff not offer pain medication.
We prefer to avoid the following medical interventions:	Artificial rupture of membranes or artificial augmentation of labor (including Pitocin during labor)
	Measures that restrict mobility (including IV and continuous or prolonged EFM)
	Episiotomy
We would appreciate:	If staffing allows, a nurse who is trained and passionate about natural childbirth
	A calm and relaxing environment
	The ability to use natural labor techniques to start, speed up, or manage labor
	Encouragement during delivery to use instinctive, natural pushing techniques and positions without time limitations
	Measures to reduce tearing (natural pushing techniques with controlled pushing at crowning, counterpressure on perineum, and warm compresses)
After our baby's birth, we prefer:	Immediate skin-to-skin contact to promote breastfeeding and bonding; mom and baby covered with blankets if necessary for warmth
	Delayed cutting of the umbilical cord (cut after pulsating has stopped)
	Postponed separation of baby and mother for routine procedures for at least 1 hour
	Newborn procedures (baby assessment, heart rate, temperature, eye ointment, vitamin K, measurements, and so on) performed on mom's chest
	Giving our baby his or her first bath
	If our child is a boy, we choose **not** to circumcise him.
We understand that no natural event can be scripted and that unforeseen circumstances occur. We have full confidence in our birth team and their professional opinions. Should a situation arise that requires deviation from our plan, we know our birth team will discuss the risks and benefits of any procedure before taking action.	
Thank you for considering and honoring our desires and supporting us in having a natural childbirth.	

Worksheet 2: Birth Preferences Checklist

Birth Plan	
Mother's Name:	
Mother's Birth Date:	Baby's Due Date:
Mother's Caregiver:	
Baby's Caregiver:	
I am writing this birth plan to help my caregiver and birthplace staff understand my wishes during my labor and birth. I have educated myself on the benefits and risks of all maternity care procedures.	
My top priority is a healthy mother and a healthy baby.	
Labor Support	During labor:
	During delivery:
Comfort Measures	☐ Walking during labor
	☐ Dim lighting
	☐ Soft music (provided by patient)
	☐ Birth ball
	☐ Doula services
	☐ Clear liquids (including water, broth, juice, Jell-O, and Popsicles) in addition to ice chips
Pain Medication	☐ Avoid pain medication.

	☐ Use pain medication as needed.
	  ☐ Offer pain medication as it becomes an option.
	  ☐ Do not offer pain medications unless requested.

	☐ Review benefits and risks before administering pain medication.
	☐ I request epidural or spinal anesthesia.
	☐ If cesarean birth is necessary, I prefer to be sedated for the postoperative repair.
	☐ If cesarean birth is necessary, I prefer to be asked if I need a sedative for the postoperative repair.
Other Interventions	☐ Avoid artificial rupture of membranes.
	☐ Avoid Pitocin if possible.
	☐ I prefer intermittent monitoring.
	☐ Use saline lock instead of IV if necessary.
	☐ Use local anesthetic before inserting saline lock or IV.
Birth	☐ Avoid episiotomy if possible.
	☐ Position a mirror so mother can observe the birth.
	☐ Permit support person to cut the umbilical cord if possible.
Early Postpartum	☐ Place baby on mother's chest immediately after birth.
	☐ Keep mother and baby skin-to-skin for at least one hour immediately after birth.
	☐ Perform necessary, time-sensitive newborn procedures on mother's chest.
	☐ Begin breastfeeding immediately after birth.
	☐ Mother and baby room together at all times.
	☐ Take baby to the nursery only at my request or in my presence.
Other Requests	
Date:	Mother's signature:

Labor Support

Continuous support from a person whose sole task is to provide emotional reassurance, physical comfort, and information can be very valuable to a laboring woman. Numerous reviews of the research show that when a woman has this kind of support from someone who is not a member of the birthplace staff or caregiver team, she is less likely to use any type of pain medication, has a lower risk of instrument delivery and cesarean surgery, and is more likely to be satisfied with her birth.[1]

For best results, your labor support person should meet as many of the following criteria as possible.

- Can be with you continuously
- Is responsible to you only
- Treats you with warmth, nurturing, and encouragement
- Is a familiar, comfortable person to you
- Knows your preferences, concerns, and priorities
- Helps you communicate with your caregiver
- Helps your partner participate in the birth
- Looks after your partner's needs
- Understands the emotional aspects of labor and works toward a positive emotional outcome
- Knows and uses comfort measures and strategies to promote labor progress
- Has a lot of experience with laboring women
- Can remain calm and objective throughout your labor

Labor Support Options

Your partner, your caregiver or labor nurse, or a close friend or relative are possible sources of labor support. But be aware of potential limitations of these people in a support role.

Your partner knows you well, cares deeply for you, and is personally invested in your birth. But your partner may find it challenging to provide the kind of support you need. He or she may be inexperienced with or uneducated about birth, may feel uncomfortable or inadequate providing labor support, or may need support as well. Or you may not have a partner.

Your caregiver or labor nurse is knowledgeable about birth and has attended many births. But those working in hospitals may be unfamiliar with the normal physiological process of labor (how labor progresses without routine interventions) or may know little about nonmedical comfort measures. In addition, a hospital-based caregiver or nurse may be very busy attending to several laboring women simultaneously. He or she is responsible not only to you, but also to other patients and to hospital protocol.

A close friend or relative knows you well and cares about you. He or she can be present continuously, can offer support to both you and your partner, and is responsible only to you. However, the average modern person—even one who has witnessed or experienced multiple births—knows little about the physiological process of birth or about nonmedical comfort measures. If you're birthing in a hospital, a friend or relative without healthcare credentials may find it challenging to provide support on the "home turf" of medical staff.

Most childbirth educators will let expectant couples bring additional support people to childbirth class. Attending classes can help a friend or relative understand the labor support person's role. Classes can also prepare such helpers to provide appropriate support.

Another way to get the best possible labor support is to hire a **birth doula**. A birth doula is a professional (usually a woman) trained in and experienced at supporting women and their partners during childbirth.

A doula meets with you before labor to get acquainted and learn about your preferences, concerns, and priorities. She joins you in labor whenever you request her presence and stays with you until about an hour after your baby's birth. Most doulas are also available for questions before labor and after birth.

A doula stays with you throughout childbirth. She offers comfort measures, gives emotional support, and suggests ways to promote labor progress. She explains what's happening in your body and helps you understand the words and actions of medical staff. She looks after your partner's needs and protects you both from unnecessary disturbances. She can also help you explain your needs and support your decisions to staff.

Hiring a Birth Doula

If you are interested in hiring a doula for your birth, ask for recommendations from your friends and relatives, your childbirth educator, and your caregiver. You can also search online at http://www.icea.org/content/member-directory.

Before hiring a birth doula, meet with her for a face-to-face interview. The following questions can help you decide whether she is a good match for you and your partner.[2]

- Could you tell me about your education, training, and experience as a birth doula?
- What is your philosophy about birth and about labor support?
- Could we meet before my due date to discuss my birth plan and your role?
- Can I call you with questions before and after my baby's birth?
- When do you try to join women in labor?
- When labor begins, do you come to our home or meet us at our birthplace?
- How long do you stay after the baby's birth?
- Are you available in the days and weeks after birth to reflect on the experience or answer questions?
- Do you have backup arrangements with another doula in case you're unavailable when my labor starts? If so, can I meet your backup doula?
- What is your fee? What does it include? Can you offer a sliding scale? Do you have a refund policy?
- Could you provide references?

Logistics

At least a month before your due date, think through the logistics of childbirth. For example, what needs to happen when you go into labor? Who and what will you need with you? Who needs to know? If you plan ahead for labor, you'll be calmer and better prepared when the journey begins.

- **Preregister at your birthplace.** If you're planning to give birth at a free-standing birth center or at home, you won't need to preregister. If you're planning a hospital birth, preregistration can save you the hassle of filling out forms while dealing with contractions. It also gives you time to read and consider hospital policies and ask questions. Many hospitals offer online preregistration. Check your hospital's website for this service. If you toured your hospital, you might have received an information packet including pre-registration forms you can mail back. You can also call the hospital and ask a customer service representative how to preregister.

- **Make plans for older children.** If you already have a child, decide—along with your partner, your caregiver, and your child—whether he or she should attend your baby's birth. (See page 36 for information on preparing your child to welcome a new baby into the family.) If your child will attend, explain the process, prepare your child for the sights and sounds he or she may witness, and suggest ways your child might help you. Pack a birth bag for your child that contains favorite books, toys, snacks, and comfort items. Also line up someone who will be dedicated to caring for your child while you're in labor. If your older child will not attend your baby's birth, arrange separate care for him or her. Explain what will happen when you go into la-bor, when and where your child may visit, and how long you might be away. Wherever your child will be during the birth, consider having a gift ready to give him or her afterward.

- **Arrange pet care.** If you have a pet, enlist a friend, relative, or neighbor to look after it during your birth and recovery. Write down instructions for feeding, exercise, veterinary emergencies, and so on.

- **Make a labor to-do list.** Write down tasks you need to do, items you need to have, and who you need to call—including phone numbers—when you go into labor.

- **Gather your birth gear.** If you're planning to give birth at a birth center or a hospital, pack a bag—or separate bags—with items you'll need during labor, items you'll need during recovery, items your partner will need, and items your baby will need. (See the Birth Bag Packing List on page 98 for suggestions.) If you're planning a home birth, assemble whatever birth gear your caregiver has asked you to provide. A home birth caregiver typically carries medical supplies and equipment, but asks families to provide things such as bed-ding, cleanup supplies, and items needed for postpartum and newborn care.

- **Plan your trip.** If you'll need to travel to your birthplace, plan your trip. Who will drive you or accompany you? Plot at least two routes to allow for different road and traffic conditions. For example, what's the best route to take at 4:00 A.M. and the best one to use at 4:00 P.M.? Do you need to con-sider any major road construction projects? Do you need to cross a bridge? If the bridge closes, what alternate route will you use? If your car breaks down, what other transportation options do you have? Keep your vehicle's gas tank full and make sure your battery is reliable. Stash some large trash bags and a few towels in your car so you can cover the seat where you'll ride.

Notes:

	Birth Bag Packing List
Mom's Items for Labor	☐ This book
	☐ Birth plan
	☐ Hospital paperwork
	☐ Purse or wallet with identification, insurance card, and cash or bank card
	☐ Two changes of birth clothing (nightgown, robe, long T-shirt, bra or camisole and sarong, or birth skirt) if you don't want to wear a hospital gown
	☐ Socks
	☐ Hair elastic, headband, kerchief, or barrette to keep your hair out of your face
	☐ Toothbrush and toothpaste
	☐ Lip balm
	☐ Snacks and drinks
	☐ Breath mints or suckers
	☐ Eyeglasses or contact lenses if needed
	☐ Essential oils
	☐ Heating pad, rice sock, or hot water bottle
	☐ Rolling pin to relieve back pain
	☐ Massaging device, massage oil, or lotion
	☐ Birth ball if your birthplace has none
	☐ Your pillow or other important comfort item
	☐ Focal point to concentrate on
	☐ Watch to time contractions
	☐ Distraction items such as cards, magazines, or DVDs
	☐ Camera or video camera
	☐ Device for listening to music
	☐ Cell phone or other mobile communication device and charger
	☐ Laptop computer
	☐ List of important phone numbers and/or e-mail addresses
	☐ Gift for older child
Mom's Items for Postpartum	☐ Robe
	☐ Slippers
	☐ Socks
	☐ Underwear and nursing bra
	☐ Nursing-friendly pajamas
	☐ Toiletries
	☐ Any medications you take regularly
	☐ Going-home clothes (mid-pregnancy size)
Your Partner's Items	☐ Wallet with cash or bank card, identification, and insurance card
	☐ Coins or small bills for vending machines
	☐ Snacks and drinks
	☐ Two changes of clothes that can be layered
	☐ Pajamas
	☐ Swimsuit to accompany you in shower or tub
	☐ Toiletries
Baby's Items	☐ Diapers (Hospitals typically supply newborn disposable diapers. Bring your own if you want to use cloth diapers or a particular kind of disposable diapers.)
	☐ One or two onesies or undershirts
	☐ One or two sleepers
	☐ Blanket
	☐ Hat
	☐ Car safety seat installed correctly in your vehicle

Chapter 7

Postpartum

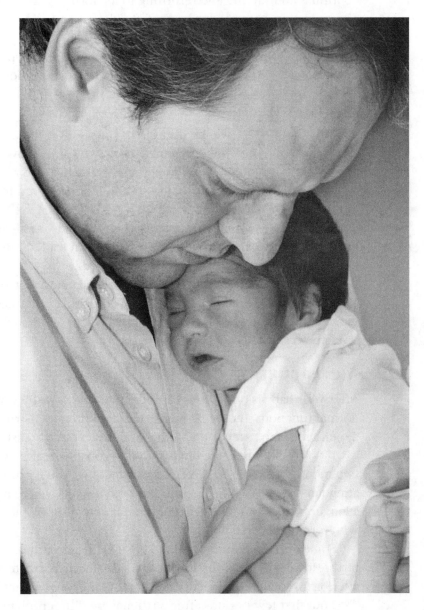

If you have your baby in a hospital, you will likely stay there one or two days after a vaginal birth or two to four days after a cesarean birth. If you have your baby at a freestanding birth center, you may be released three to eight hours after giving birth. If you have your baby at home, your caregiver will probably leave within a similar timeframe.

After having your baby and leaving your birthplace—or saying good-bye to your caregiver—you may feel as if you've traveled to another dimension. Many new parents say that the whole world looks different after their baby is born.

Indeed, your world changes dramatically when you become a parent. This chapter provides a primer on the physical and mental adjustments mothers experience in the first few months after giving birth.

Uterine Changes

Afterpains

You may feel afterpains (see page 64) for a week or so after birth, as your uterus continues contracting and returning to its normal size. Many women notice that afterpains are stronger during breastfeeding, because breastfeeding stimulates uterine contractions.

Slow breathing may help you relax through the afterpains. If you find them bothersome, your caregiver may want you to try ibuprofen.

Lochia

For about four to six weeks after birth, your body will continue to expel lochia. (See page 64.) At first it will resemble heavy menstrual flow, possibly with clots. The quantity of lochia should decrease gradually, and clots should cease. In addition, the color of your lochia should fade from red to brown or pink to tan, yellow, or white.

Wear pads—first maternity pads, then thinner ones—to absorb the flow of lochia. Do not wear tampons, because they can lead to infection when used before you're completely recovered from birth.

If your lochia develops a foul odor, this may be a sign of infection. Call your caregiver for advice. If you notice that your lochia is increasing or turning redder, this may be a sign of overexertion. Make an effort to reduce your activity level and rest more often.

Menstruation

After your baby is born, your reproductive system will eventually resume its normal functions, including menstruation. When menstruation returns will depend to some extent on whether and how you're breastfeeding.

If you're not breastfeeding, you will probably begin menstruating one to two months after birth. If you're breastfeeding, you'll probably start menstruating later. If you're nursing your baby exclusively, you're more likely to have a longer break from menstruation than if you're supplementing breastfeeding with formula feeding.

Some nursing mothers begin menstruating as early as two months after birth. However, many nursing mothers do not menstruate for several months after birth. Some do not menstruate for a year or two, or until their children wean.

Your first few periods after birth may be different than usual. They may be heavier and longer or lighter and shorter than your periods were before pregnancy. Eventually they'll return to normal.

Perineal Healing

If you had a vaginal birth, your perineum may be sore for a few weeks. You may have received stitches to repair a tear or episiotomy. Or your perineum may be swollen or bruised. Use the following tips to help your perineum heal and to reduce discomfort.

- During the first few days after birth, use ice packs occasionally to reduce pain and swelling. To make an ice pack, fill a plastic zipper bag with crushed ice and wrap it in paper toweling or in a clean, lightweight cloth. Or pour witch hazel on a sanitary pad and freeze it. Hold the ice pack in place with your maternity pad.
- Take a bath in a clean tub. Sit in warm or cool water—whichever feels better—for ten to twenty minutes.
- Keep your perineum clean and dry between ice packs and baths to avoid infection.
- When you're having a bowel movement, gently press toilet paper on your perineum to support the tender tissues and prevent stretching. Wipe carefully from front to back to avoid spreading germs from your rectum to your perineum. After you urinate, pour or squirt warm water over your perineum to clean the area. Gently pat it dry with toilet paper from front to back.
- Lie down to rest as often as possible to neutralize the effects of gravity and help reduce swelling.
- Do not douche. Douching, like tampon use, raises your risk of infection.
- If sitting is painful, you may find it more comfortable to sit on firm surfaces than on soft ones. Sit down slowly, one buttock at a time. You might also try sitting on a donut-shaped pillow or a rolled towel formed into a donut shape.
- Do Kegel exercises (see page 11) to improve circulation, reduce swelling, promote healing, and strengthen your pelvic floor muscles.
- If you had a large episiotomy or tore severely, you may have intense pain at first. Take enough pain medication to be comfortable.
- If your pain is worsening, or if your tear or incision doesn't seem to be healing, call your caregiver for advice.

Bladder and Bowel Changes

Bladder Function

During the first day or so after birth, you may have trouble urinating. This difficulty may be a result of tearing, bruising, or swelling. Pain medication may be interfering with your bladder's signals to your brain. Or you may simply be afraid to urinate, dreading that it will hurt.

To solve this problem, try the following tips. If you still can't urinate after trying these strategies, consult your caregiver.

- Drink plenty of fluids.
- Relax or bulge your perineum while you're using the toilet.
- Pour warm water over your perineum while you're trying to urinate.
- Try to urinate while showering.

After resolving any initial difficulty, you may find yourself using the bathroom a lot. In early postpartum, your body expels extra fluids through urination.

Some women experience urinary incontinence after giving birth. Urinary incontinence is involuntary urine leakage. Leaking commonly occurs when a new mother coughs, sneezes, exercises, or has a full bladder. For most women, postpartum urinary incontinence resolves in a few weeks without treatment.

Notes:

Notes:

If you're experiencing urinary incontinence, you can take the following steps to address the problem.

- Do Kegel exercises often. (See page 11.)
- Wear a pad to protect your clothes.
- Talk with your caregiver about incontinence if it lasts more than two months.

Bowel Function

During the first several days after birth, you may have trouble moving your bowels. Constipation may be a result of iron supplements, pain medication, digestive sluggishness left over from pregnancy, stretched abdominal muscles, perineal pain, or rectal pain from hemorrhoids. (See page 11 for more information on hemorrhoids.)

To prevent or treat constipation, use the following strategies. If you remain constipated after trying these strategies, consult your caregiver.

- Eat a fiber-rich diet including fresh and dried fruits, vegetables, and whole grains.
- Add 1 tablespoon of flax meal to your food. Flax meal is ground flaxseed. Most natural-food stores carry flaxseed and flax meal.
- Drink plenty of water.
- If you're taking an iron supplement, take it with food, try a different brand, or take smaller doses more often throughout the day.
- Move your bowels promptly when you feel the urge to do so.
- To avoid causing or aggravating hemorrhoids, don't strain during bowel movements.
- Try an over-the-counter high-fiber product, such as Metamucil.
- Ask your caregiver to recommend a stool softener.
- With your caregiver's approval, exercise regularly.

Some women develop hemorrhoids (see page 11) during pregnancy, and the problem persists after birth. Some women develop hemorrhoids during a vaginal birth. For most women, postpartum hemorrhoids resolve in a month or so without treatment.

To prevent or treat postpartum hemorrhoids, try the following tips. If these strategies don't help, or if your hemorrhoids persist beyond a month postpartum, consult your caregiver.

- Prevent constipation. (See above.)
- Apply witch hazel or products that contain it to the area.
- Soak in a warm bath for ten to twenty minutes.
- Avoid heavy lifting.
- Do Kegel exercises. (See page 11.)
- Don't strain during bowel movements.

Some women experience fecal incontinence after giving birth. Fecal incontinence is involuntary leakage of gas or stool. For most women, postpartum fecal incontinence resolves in a few weeks without treatment.

If you're experiencing fecal incontinence, you can take the following steps to address the problem.

- Do Kegel exercises often. (See page 11.)
- Wear a pad to protect your clothes.
- Talk with your caregiver about incontinence if it lasts more than two months.

Cesarean Recovery

If you gave birth by cesarean, you face extra postpartum adjustment. You will experience most of the typical physical changes, such as lochia, afterpains, bladder and bowel adjustment, milk engorgement, and fatigue. Like all new mothers, you'll be adjusting to life with a baby. In addition, you'll be recovering from major surgery. You'll have pain at your incision site as well as abdominal pain and weakness.

The two most helpful things you can do to speed your recovery after a cesarean are controlling your pain and resting adequately. By the time you leave the hospital, you will be taking oral pain medications. Take enough to stay comfortable. Controlling your pain enables you to get enough rest, move about, and care for your baby.

The more rest you get during your first two weeks at home, the faster you'll feel better. Forgo household chores and most other normal activities at first. Avoid lifting anything besides your baby. Gradually increase your physical activity. Regular, gentle movement will help you not only regain your strength, but also avoid constipation and gas pain. Start with short, slow walks. Climb stairs carefully when you feel steady enough to do so. Don't drive until you've stopped taking prescription pain medication and feel physically capable of controlling your vehicle. Delay sexual intercourse for two to four weeks.

To help your incision heal, protect it and keep it clean and dry. When you nurse your baby, place a pillow on your lap to cushion your incision. When you bathe or shower, gently clean your incision with soap and pat it dry thoroughly. Wear soft, loose clothing that won't rub or otherwise irritate your incision. Make sure air can circulate around the incision. Let the surgical tape covering your incision come off on its own.

You may feel sharp pain, burning, itching, prickling, numbness, pulling, or other discomfort at your incision site for a few months. After the incision heals, you may notice that it has a firm ridge of scar tissue. Call your caregiver if your incision becomes hot, hard, red, sore, open, or draining.

Rest and Activity

After you have a baby, you face a peculiar challenge. In order to feel well physically and mentally, you need to get both sufficient rest and sufficient exercise. And somehow, you need to balance these personal needs with your baby's constant needs.

If that sounds impossible to you, you're not alone. Most new parents feel overwhelmed. Their babies take up nearly every minute of every day. The unclaimed minutes offer precious little time for sleeping, eating, and showering—much less exercising, cleaning, or doing just about anything else.

You can achieve a healthy balance with a little effort. Make it a priority to get rest and exercise each day. Remember that caring for yourself helps you take good care of your baby.

Notes:

Rest

Fatigue and sleep deprivation make your body feel awful and your emotions bleak. The following strategies can help you get enough rest to recover physically and feel positive about your new parenting role.

- Make sleeping your top priority after meeting your baby's needs. Fight the temptation to do too much. Let all other tasks go until you've gotten enough rest.
- Limit the number of visitors you have and the length of each visitor's stay.
- Try to sleep when your baby sleeps.
- To remind yourself to rest, stay in your pajamas for the first week or two postpartum. Or stay in your pajamas—and in bed—each day until you've gotten enough sleep to function well.
- Sleep with your baby close by so you don't have to strain to hear him or her, and you don't have to get up for feedings. If your baby's noise or proximity keeps you awake, have someone else care for him or her while you try to sleep.
- To save you time and effort, keep a supply of clothes, diapers, and other necessities wherever you spend a lot of time, such as next to your bed or the couch.
- Care for your baby in shifts with your partner.
- Do anything that helps you relax, such as taking a bath, reading a few pages of a novel, listening to music, eating a particular snack, or doing relaxation exercises.
- If necessary, take enough pain medication to be comfortable.

Activity

Daily exercise can help restore muscle strength and firm up your body. Exercise can also raise your energy level and improve your sense of well-being. Use the following strategies to help you develop a daily routine of appropriate postpartum exercise.

- First let your body rest and recover for a week or two postpartum.
- When you feel up to it, discuss with your caregiver your desire to start an exercise program. Find out whether you've recovered enough physically to begin gentle exercise.
- Ask your caregiver to recommend activities to do and to avoid. Start with a type and level of exercise that's easy for you. Slowly build up to more strenuous exercise.
- Consider starting your exercise routine with walking. Walking is easy to do nearly anywhere, anytime. It's cheap, too; all you need is a pair of comfortable shoes. You can do it with your baby, and it provides both of you with fresh air and a change of scenery. In addition, walking helps prepare your body for more vigorous exercise.
- Find out whether your local health club, community center, college, hospital, or other facility offers a postpartum exercise class.
- Whenever you exercise, begin with five to ten minutes of warm-up and stretching. Follow this with twenty to thirty minutes of exercise. End with five to ten minutes of cool-down and stretching. Warming up and cooling down will help you avoid injuries and sore muscles.
- While you exercise, wear cool, comfortable clothing and a well-fitting bra.
- Drink plenty of water before and after your workout.
- Listen to your body when you exercise. Don't overdo it. If you're exhausted, in pain, or notice that your lochia is increasing or becoming redder, you're probably overexerting yourself. Stop exercising and consult your caregiver before you resume your exercise routine.

Sex and Contraception

Chances are, neither you nor your partner has much interest in sex during the first weeks postpartum. Fatigue, soreness, hormonal changes, and newborn demands dampen the libidos of many new parents.

Most caregivers advise abstaining from sex for six weeks after birth. But if you and your partner feel ready, if your perineum has healed, and if your lochia is dwindling, let your caregiver know you both feel ready.

Talk openly and respectfully with your partner about your desires. Choose the right time together. Show love and affection in other ways if you're not yet ready for sex.

Whenever you choose to resume sexual intercourse, take it slow and easy. You may still be sore, and breastfeeding hormones may cause vaginal dryness. Use a water-soluble lubricant if necessary. If vaginal or perineal pain gets worse over time or lasts longer than six months, consult your caregiver.

Remember that you can become pregnant anytime you have intercourse—even shortly after birth, and even if you're not yet menstruating. If you wish to avoid another pregnancy at this time, talk with your caregiver about your contraception options.

Milk may leak or spray from your breasts during sex. Keep your sense of humor and a towel handy.

Breast Care

As soon as your baby is born, your breasts gear up for breastfeeding. For the first one to three days postpartum, your breasts produce colostrum. Colostrum is a yellowish, highly nutritious "first milk" your body makes. Your breasts begin to produce whitish mature milk between the second and fifth days. When your mature milk comes in, your breasts may become engorged, or painfully swollen. (For more information on breastfeeding, see pages 28–30 and 120–123.)

If you're not breastfeeding, take the following steps to reduce discomfort and milk production. Engorgement usually subsides by the end of the first week postpartum.

- During a warm shower, circle one breast with both hands. Compress gently, moving the milk forward and out of the breast. Express just enough milk to make you comfortable. Repeat this process on your other breast. Express a little milk in this way whenever you feel uncomfortably engorged.
- Apply ice packs to your breasts for twenty minutes every four hours. This strategy can relieve both pain and swelling.
- If necessary, take acetaminophen or ibuprofen for pain relief.
- Avoid breast stimulation, which signals your breasts to produce milk.
- Place cool, raw green cabbage leaves against your breasts. For reasons that are not fully understood, this treatment helps some women with engorgement.

If your baby has died, consider whether you would find it more helpful to suppress lactation or to pump and donate your milk in honor of your baby. (See page 90 for more information on neonatal illness and death.)

Notes:

Emotions

The first few weeks after having a baby can be physically and emotionally challenging. Hormonal fluctuation plus the stress of parenting a newborn can equal mood swings. Other factors can contribute to postpartum emotional challenges, too. Isolation; lack of sleep; routine changes; depression or anxiety during pregnancy; disappointment with or trauma from the birth; a sick baby; financial problems; or a history of depression, anxiety, or posttraumatic stress disorder can increase your risk for depression and other mood disorders.

Encourage people who know you well to watch for unusual behaviors. If you are unable or unwilling to request help, they must do it for you. Ask your caregiver to recommend local support groups for new mothers.

Baby Blues

About 80 percent of women experience a condition called baby blues after birth. Baby blues usually begin between the third and fifth days postpartum. The symptoms of baby blues are:

- Crying easily
- Occasional sadness
- Difficulty sleeping
- Irritability
- Mild anxiety, usually about the baby
- Tiredness
- Difficulty concentrating
- Feeling overwhelmed
- Feeling out of control
- Low self-confidence

Baby blues are common. For most women, the feeling is mild and temporary, lasting less than two weeks. If you have baby blues, you can feel better by resting as much as possible, controlling your pain, napping when you can, and asking friends and family for more support. For a few women, baby blues develop into more serious emotional disorders. Some women experience baby blues when they wean their babies (stop breastfeeding), due to hormonal fluctuations.

Postpartum Mood Disorders

About 20 percent of women experience a family of conditions called postpartum mood disorders (PPMDs). These conditions occur more often in women who have a history of depression, anxiety, or psychological trauma. PPMDs can begin any time during the first year postpartum. They can last indefinitely without treatment. The symptoms of postpartum mood disorders are:

- Constant sadness and crying
- Despair
- Apathy
- Extremely low self-esteem
- Major sleep disturbance
- Exhaustion and lack of energy
- Loss of appetite or overeating
- Moderate to severe anxiety
- Outbursts of anger
- Inability to care for self or baby
- Obsessive thoughts or rituals (thoughts or actions that preoccupy you and won't go away), such as constant hand washing, housecleaning, checking on baby, or checking locks
- Panic attacks (fast heartbeat, sweaty palms, shortness of breath, choking sensation, lightheadedness, chest pain, nausea, diarrhea, and/or sense of unreality)
- Fear of being alone, of dying, of leaving home, of hurting baby, of being a bad mother, and/or of germs
- Extreme mood elevation followed by long-term depression
- Preoccupation with traumatic event, flashbacks, recurrent nightmares, and/or extreme protectiveness of self or baby
- Thoughts about hurting or killing self or baby

If you have any of these symptoms, the best thing you can do to feel better is to acknowledge them. Postpartum mood disorders are surprisingly common and are nothing to be ashamed of. But if you can't eat, sleep, or take care of yourself or your baby, or if you have thoughts about hurting yourself or your baby, you should get professional help. You face a higher risk of postpartum depression if you had a difficult birth or if you are formula feeding.

Professional help for postpartum mood disorders may include:

- Discussing your symptoms with your caregiver.
- Getting counseling with a therapist or psychiatrist who specializes in PPMDs. Cognitive therapy and interpersonal psychotherapy are particularly effective for PPMDs.
- Taking prescribed medication for anxiety, obsessive-compulsive disorder (OCD), depression, and bipolar disorder.
- Attending a PPMDs support group. To find a local support group, ask your caregiver, childbirth educator, hospital, or public health department or contact Postpartum Support International by phone (800-944-4773) or online at http://postpartum.net.

In addition, the following self-care steps may help you treat a postpartum mood disorder:

- Educate yourself about PPMDs.
- Eat a balanced, nutritious diet (see page 6), including adequate omega-3 fatty acids and vitamin D. Research shows that deficiencies of these nutrients can contribute to mood disorders.[1]
- Get regular exercise. (See page 7.)
- Get enough sleep and rest. (See page 104.)
- Set aside at least a few minutes for yourself each day.
- Avoid caffeine, alcohol, and sleep medication.
- Get plenty of sunshine and fresh air.

Postpartum Psychosis

Less than 1 percent of women (about 1 in every 1,000 to 2,000 women) experience a condition called postpartum psychosis. Postpartum psychosis is the most serious form of postpartum mood disorders. It usually begins soon after birth and often appears first as major depression. The most common type of postpartum psychosis is postpartum bipolar disorder with psychosis. The symptoms of postpartum psychosis are:

- Not sleeping for two to three days: This is often an early symptom of psychosis. It is serious and requires immediate medical attention.
- Severe agitation
- Mood swings
- Depression
- Delusions

Postpartum psychosis is a very serious illness and requires immediate psychiatric treatment. Treatment may include hospitalization, ongoing psychotherapy, and medication.

Notes:

Notes:

Warning Signs

Most women experience a healthy and uncomplicated recovery from childbirth. But it's important to know the signs of a potential problem. If you experience any of the following symptoms, call your caregiver immediately so he or she can help you assess the situation and, if appropriate, begin treatment promptly.

- **Fever of 100.4°F (38°C) or higher** may be a sign of infection of the uterus, urinary tract, breast, perineal incision or tear, or cesarean incision, or it may be a sign of another illness.
- **A red, hot, painful area on the breast with fever and aches** may be a sign of a breast infection.
- **Blood in the urine or burning during urination** may be a sign of a urinary tract infection.
- **Vaginal soreness, itching, or foul-smelling discharge** may be a sign of infection of the uterus or vagina.
- **Increased perineal pain and/or pus-like or foul-smelling discharge from perineal incision or tear** may be a sign of infection or reopening of the incision or tear.
- **Opening of and/or blood or pus-like discharge from cesarean incision** may be a sign of infection of the incision.
- **Any sudden new pain** may be a sign of uterine infection or reopening of an incision or tear.
- **Inability to urinate** may be a sign of swelling around or damage to the urethra.
- **Passing a blood clot larger than a lemon and/or any bleeding heavy enough to soak a maxi pad in an hour** may be a sign of retained placenta or uterine infection.
- **A swollen, red, hot, and tender area on the leg** may be a sign of a blood clot in a blood vessel.
- **Rash or hives** may be a sign of allergic reaction to medication.
- **Severe headache that's worse when you're upright** may be a sign of a spinal headache caused by epidural or spinal anesthesia.
- **Pain and tenderness in the pelvis, difficulty walking, and a grating sensation in the pelvis** may be a sign of separation of the cartilage between your pubic bones.
- **Severe anxiety, panic, or depression; uncontrollable crying; rage; fast heartbeat; inability to eat or sleep; or difficulty breathing** may be a sign of a postpartum mood disorder.
- **Verbal or physical abuse by or fear of your partner** may be a sign of domestic violence (see page 13).

Chapter 8
Newborn Care

Chances are, you're not the only member of your family feeling a little disoriented after childbirth. Your baby, too, has just made an amazing journey.

Your baby enters the world nearly helpless to meet his or her own needs. That job is yours, of course. This chapter offers a basic guide to caring for your newborn.

Newborn Procedures

Regardless of your birthplace, your baby will likely undergo various procedures in the first days of life. The following paragraphs describe common newborn procedures. All can and should be done in the mother's room or in the parents' presence.

Birth Certificate

A birth certificate is an official document that records the birth of a child at a specific time, in a specific place, to a specific parent or set of parents. It establishes a child's public identity by documenting his or her age, name, family ties, and nationality. It opens the door to accessing public and private services, such as education, health care, licensing, voting, and more.

For most births, the birthplace or caregiver supplies a birth certificate form. Parents fill out part of the form. The birthplace or caregiver completes the rest and sends it to the proper government agency. The agency stores the record.

Parents must register unassisted births or those attended by unlicensed midwives. The process varies by location. Contact your state or provincial department of vital statistics to find out how to register your baby's birth.

Blood Screening

All U.S. states and Canadian provinces require some newborn blood screening, so birthplaces and maternity caregivers routinely perform this screening. A caregiver typically draws blood from your baby's heel or vein between the second and seventh day after birth. Then a lab screens the blood for various genetic, metabolic, or hormonal disorders. Screening determines the baby's risk of having a particular disorder. It does not detect the presence of the disorder itself. The diseases screened for vary by location. They are all rare. But early screening for them is important because without early treatment, they can cause lifelong physical problems, mental retardation, or death.

Hearing Screening

Most North American states and provinces also require newborn hearing screening. About half of babies with hearing problems have no known risk factors, so newborn screening is important for all babies. It's especially important for premature babies, those with family histories of hearing problems, and those who've come in contact with organisms or medications that raise the risk of hearing loss.

Without newborn hearing screening, most babies with hearing problems get diagnosed after fourteen months.[1] By this time, language development is already delayed. As a result, a child is more likely to perform below grade level, be held back, or drop out of school. In contrast, children diagnosed early get early intervention. Most function at peer level by the time they start school.

A caregiver typically tests your baby's hearing between the second and seventh day after birth. The test is painless and noninvasive. While your baby is sleeping, the caregiver places a tiny soft device in your baby's ear and may place electrodes on your baby's head. The caregiver then measures how your baby's inner ear and/or brain activity responds to sounds.

Don't be alarmed if you're asked to repeat the hearing screening. Amniotic fluid in a newborn's ear canal can affect the results of the initial screening.

Jaundice Screening and Treatment

Jaundice is a buildup of bilirubin in the blood. Bilirubin is a substance created when red blood cells break down.

Each day some red blood cells in the human body break down. As they do, reddish hemoglobin (an oxygen-carrying chemical in the blood) changes to yellowish bilirubin. The liver filters out bilirubin and changes it into a form that can pass out of the body via bowel movements.

If a person's blood contains too much bilirubin, the skin or the whites of the eyes turn yellow. If bilirubin is very high, it can enter the brain and cause brain damage.

Newborns are vulnerable to jaundice because more red blood cells break down right after birth than at other times, and a newborn's immature liver may have trouble keeping up with bilirubin removal. About 60 percent of newborns experience some degree of jaundice. Babies face a higher risk of jaundice when mothers have gestational diabetes, induced labor, pain medication, or instrument delivery.

If your baby's skin or eyes seem yellow, a caregiver may order a test to check your baby's bilirubin level. The test may be a blood test or use of a jaundice meter, which estimates bilirubin level by flashing a light on your baby's forehead.

Most babies with jaundice have it mildly. Their bilirubin levels drop without treatment.

If your baby's bilirubin is high enough to cause concern, treatment may include the following:
- Increasing the number of feedings to encourage bilirubin excretion
- Phototherapy (exposing baby's skin to a special light that helps change bilirubin to an easily excreted form)

Circumcision

If you've decided to have your baby boy circumcised, discuss the procedure with your baby's caregiver beforehand. Find out whether the caregiver uses anesthesia for pain relief. Newborns feel pain, and circumcision is painful without anesthesia.

The procedure may take place on the second day after birth. Here's what happens: Your baby's caregiver lays him on his back in a special bed and secures his body and limbs with straps or by swaddling him. The caregiver should then give your baby an injection of anesthesia to numb the penis.

After the anesthesia takes effect, the caregiver washes your baby's penis with antiseptic to kill germs. The caregiver surgically removes the foreskin. Some babies cry and are upset. Others may sleep through the procedure. After the caregiver removes the foreskin, he or she covers the area with gauze coated in petroleum jelly. Then your baby is diapered.

Skin-to-skin contact, breastfeeding, and expressed breast milk can comfort your baby after any painful procedure. Your baby may not feed as well for a few hours after the operation. (See page 117 for instructions on caring for a circumcised penis.)

Notes:

Baby Care Basics

The following paragraphs explain the basic behaviors and needs of babies. You'll also learn how to meet these needs and cope with common baby-care challenges.

You may find the task overwhelming at first. This is a normal reaction; don't let it get you down. Soon you'll be an expert in understanding and caring for your baby.

Sleeping and Waking

Babies born after unmedicated labors are very alert after birth. If you had pain medication in labor, your baby may be groggy or drowsy for several hours or even days. You may have to work hard to wake him or her.

During the first several months of life, it's normal for babies to get their sleep in many short stretches throughout the day and night. A baby's typical sleep cycle is about sixty to ninety minutes long—similar in length to the typical infant hunger cycle. Some babies have a two- to four-hour stretch of sleep once per day. Longer sleep periods, or multiple long stretches of sleep per day, are unusual. They can interfere with weight gain, growth, and development. Research shows that the idea that babies should sleep through the night is unrealistic at best and damaging at worst.[2]

Babies spend their days and nights moving through six states of consciousness in cycles about sixty to ninety minutes long:

1. **Deep sleep:** Your baby breathes rhythmically and lies still, quiet, and calm. Your baby may occasionally jerk or suckle, but is mostly relaxed. Loud noises fail to wake your baby. Much healing and growth takes place during deep sleep. This state offers you a good chance to rest or do necessary tasks.

2. **Light sleep:** Your baby breathes irregularly, moves his or her body and face, and makes sounds. Your baby's eyes move rapidly beneath closed eyelids. He or she may respond to noises, touch, light, and motion. This state may be a break between periods of deep sleep or a transition between deep sleep and drowsiness. If your baby moves about or makes noises during this state, wait a moment to see whether he or she is waking or moving into deep sleep.

3. **Drowsiness:** Your baby acts sleepy. His or her eyes may cross or roll back under drooping eyelids. Your baby breathes irregularly and may stretch, yawn, or startle. He or she responds to sensory stimulation. Your baby passes through drowsiness while waking up or falling asleep. Sometimes you can help your baby fall asleep again by nursing, holding, or rocking him or her. You can help your baby wake up by picking up or talking to him or her.

4. **Quiet alert:** Your baby is wide-awake and alert. He or she is still and calm, looking at you and breathing rhythmically. Your baby is attentive and responsive to his or her surroundings. This state offers a good opportunity for play and interaction. Much learning takes place during the quiet alert state.

5. **Active alert:** Your baby is awake and agitated. He or she moves about, makes faces, and breathes irregularly. Your baby may fuss, suck on his or her fingers, or make mouthing movements. This state shows that your baby needs something—probably food. Try nursing first. If nursing is not helpful, your baby may be tired, overstimulated, bored, lonely, cold, hot, wet, or sick. In any case, your baby needs comforting before he or she panics and enters the crying state.

6. **Crying:** Your baby flails about, makes faces, breathes irregularly, cries, and may scream. He or she is irritable and unreceptive. Crying shows that your

baby has an unmet need and can't cope anymore. He or she needs comfort, which usually means being fed and held. Crying is hard on babies and can even be damaging. Never let your baby "cry it out." Always hold or gently try to comfort a crying baby. If you feel desperate to quiet your baby, call another adult for help!

Many babies need a lot of holding and nursing in the late afternoon and evening. Some take a long nap around lunchtime. You can try to schedule your daily activities around your baby's habits. However, be aware that your baby's pattern will likely change as he or she grows.

Grooming

Bathing

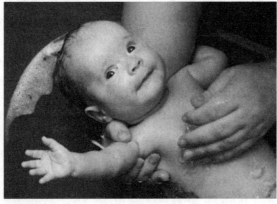

If you keep your baby's face, hands, and bottom clean, frequent bathing isn't necessary. In fact, too much bathing can dry your baby's skin. One or two baths per week suffice until your baby becomes a crawling, food-eating mess maker.

In the past, caregivers recommended sponge baths until a baby's umbilicus heals. However, newer research shows that immersion in water does not raise the risk of umbilical infection in healthy newborns. Furthermore, babies tend to stay warmer—and parents enjoy the experience more—during immersion than during sponge baths.[3]

To give your baby a tub bath, fill a sink or baby tub with a few inches of clean, warm water. Place a clean washcloth, some very mild soap (optional), and a clean towel nearby. Lower your naked baby into the water. First wash your baby's face with water. Then wash the rest of your baby's body with soap and water, ending with the diaper area. If your baby has hair, gently massage it with a bit of soap. Rinse off the soap with clear, warm water. Carefully lift out your slippery baby and wrap him or her in a towel.

To bathe with your baby, fill your bathtub with several inches of clean, warm water. Place a clean washcloth, some very mild soap (optional), and a towel for you nearby. Lay your naked, towel-wrapped baby in an infant seat near the tub. Undress and sit in the tub. Then unwrap your baby and lay him or her back on your thighs. First wash your baby's face with water. Then wash the rest of your baby's body with soap and water, ending with the diaper area. If your baby has hair, gently massage it with a bit of soap. Rinse off the soap with clear, warm water. Carefully lift out your slippery baby and place him or her in the infant seat, wrapped in a towel. Get out of the tub and dry off.

Do not try to clean the inside of your baby's nose or ears. Clean the outside only, and the little hairs in the ears and nose will move wax and mucus out. Never use cotton swabs. These can damage your baby's delicate ears and nose.

Do not use products such as baby powder, baby lotion, or baby oil. Your baby can breathe in airborne powder particles and become sick. In addition, baby powder may encourage yeast growth. Lotions and oils may encourage the growth of bad bacteria on your baby's skin.

After a bath, pat your baby dry thoroughly with a towel. Then dress him or her. If necessary, groom your baby's hair with a soft-bristle brush or wide-tooth comb.

Dressing

Dress your newborn as you would dress, in the same number of layers as you are wearing. Resist the urge to overdress your baby. Overheating is a risk factor for sudden infant death syndrome (SIDS). SIDS is the death of an apparently healthy infant, usually before one year of age, due to an unknown cause and occurring especially during sleep. (See page 119 for more information.) The only extra precautions to dressing are as follows:

- **Heat loss:** Newborns lose a lot of heat from their heads, which are relatively large and often bald. In cold weather or a drafty building, keep your baby close to your body and consider putting a warm hat on his or her head.
- **Sun protection:** Baby skin is very sensitive to sunlight, and newborns should not wear chemical sunscreens until they are at least six months old. A little sun is a good thing, but sunburns are painful and damaging. Buy sunscreen for babies and read the directions carefully. Keep your baby out of direct sun to avoid sunburn. Use lightweight, light-colored clothing with long sleeves and long legs, a sun hat, and sunshades as needed. Even when your baby is in the shade, he or she may be exposed to reflected sunlight. Check your baby often and reapply sunscreen as needed.

If overdressed, your baby feels hot or sweaty all over and may have a heat rash (tiny pink pimples on the shoulders, trunk, and neck). If underdressed, your baby's hands, feet, and back feel cold and may be blue or mottled. If dressed appropriately, your baby's body feels warm while his or her hands and feet feel cool.

When you dress your baby, guide each body part gently through the proper opening. Clothes that pull on from the bottom or fasten up the front are easy to put on babies. Pullover garments are trickier because babies' heads are big.

To put a pullover garment on your baby, first stretch the neck hole. Support your baby's head with one hand. With the other hand, pull the shirt over your baby's head from back to front. Reach into each sleeve from the wrist opening and grasp your baby's hand. Gently pull your baby's arm through the sleeve. Reverse this process when removing a pullover garment.

Your baby does not need shoes. Shoes can interfere with normal foot development. Use booties and socks until well after your baby begins walking, when he or she may need shoes for foot protection outdoors.

Nail Care

A newborn's fingernails and toenails grow fast. And with poor limb control, a baby can easily end up with a face full of scratches. To trim your baby's nails, you can:

- **Cut or clip:** This method works best with a partner. In a well-lit place, one person can snuggle the baby while the other trims baby's nails with baby nail scissors or clippers. Press the fingertip away from the nail to avoid nicks, and hold your baby's hand firmly as you clip.
- **File:** If you have the time and your baby has the patience, you can file his or her nails with an emery board.

To minimize wiggling, many parents trim nails while their babies are sleeping, nursing, or otherwise distracted. Some parents trim their babies' nails by nibbling them. This method can spread germs from a parent's mouth to any scrapes or scratches in the baby's skin.

Elimination

Urination

During the first week of life, your newborn should have at least one wet diaper for each day of his or her age—one wet diaper on day one, two wet diapers on day two, and so on. As your milk production increases, urine output also increases. Expect six to eight—or more—wet diapers per day by the end of the first week.

Bowel Movements

Babies should pass their first bowel movement on the first day. This is a sticky, greenish-black stool called meconium. On day two, your baby may not have a bowel movement at all, or may pass a small dark or greenish stool. On day three, stools increase in volume and may begin turning yellow. If your baby has not had a bowel movement by day three, contact your baby's caregiver right away.

For a breastfed baby, expect to see four yellow, loose, seedy stools on day four. From day five through week six, your baby should have three to five—or more—loose yellow stools per day. A breastfed newborn may have a bowel movement after each feeding or may have a few large bowel movements per day. After about six weeks, bowel movements may be less frequent, and the stools may be thicker—more like toothpaste. Older breastfed babies may even go several days between bowel movements.

A formula-fed baby should have bowel movements one or two times per day after the first week of life. If your baby is formula-fed, he or she will have putty-like stools.

Constipation is a condition in which the body produces hard, dry poop that's difficult to pass. This condition is very rare in breastfed babies, because human milk is so easy for babies to digest. It's more common in formula-fed babies. Formula is harder to digest than breast milk.

Diarrhea is a condition in which the body produces excessive watery stools. This condition, too, is more common in formula-fed babies than breastfed ones. If your baby has diarrhea, he or she may have very watery bowel movements more often than usual. Your baby's stool may contain mucus or traces of blood and may smell awful. Your baby may look sick or act weak. If your baby shows symptoms of diarrhea, consult his or her caregiver. Diarrhea can lead to dehydration. Continue breastfeeding if your baby has diarrhea. Your milk is even more important when your baby is sick.

Waste Management

One way or another, you'll need to manage all the urine and stool your baby produces. You can do so with cloth diapers, disposable diapers, or a diaper-free method called elimination communication (EC).

Cloth diapers come in many designs and materials. The diapers may be cotton, hemp, or fleece. The covers may be soft and stretchy wool, coated polyester with snaps or Velcro, or vinyl with elastic openings. Some cloth diapers are contoured. Others are simple rectangles. Some diapers have snaps or pockets for attaching absorbent liners. Some cloth diapers have an attached cover. Others can be used with any cover. Some cloth diapers are adjustable, so a baby can wear them into toddlerhood. Others come in age-tailored sizes. If you live in a city, you may have access to shops that sell cloth diapers or a diaper

Notes:

delivery-and-laundering service. No matter where you live, you can use the Internet to buy cloth diapers from scores of family-owned businesses. To learn more about cloth diapers, visit http://mothering.com/diapering.

Disposable diapers are widely available in stores. They are more absorbent than cloth diapers. However, they are more expensive over time, and they produce a lot of garbage. Some parents worry about exposing their babies to the chemicals in disposable diapers, some of which are linked to health problems. In addition, bleaches, dyes, and perfumes used in disposable diapers can cause irritation. Some manufacturers minimize the health and environmental impacts of disposable diapers by using biodegradable and/or hypoallergenic materials.

Parents who practice elimination communication learn and watch for cues that indicate their baby needs to urinate or have a bowel movement. Some parents develop a toileting cue to communicate with their children about toileting. On cue, the parent holds the baby over a sink (for urine only) or the toilet or a special potty (for a bowel movement). To facilitate EC, parents dress their babies for easy access to baby's bottom. Some parents begin EC immediately, while others wait a few weeks or months. Some parents use EC full-time, while others practice it part-time. Advantages of EC include enhanced communication between parents and babies, reduced diapering costs, minimal health and environmental impacts, and earlier toilet learning. Drawbacks include time and energy investment and more frequent messes, especially at first. To learn more about EC, visit http://www.diaperfreebaby.org.

Health Care

Skin Care

Newborn skin is delicate and sensitive. A few simple strategies can help you keep your baby's skin healthy.

- If your baby is born with vernix on his or skin, don't wash it off. Vernix helps your baby stay hydrated and fight infections.
- Bathe your baby no more than twice a week to avoid stripping the skin of natural protective oils.
- Use water only on your baby's skin for the first month.
- Choose baby-care products carefully to avoid toxins. For help with this task, visit http://www.cosmeticsdatabase.com.
- Wash your baby's clothing and bedding with fragrance- and dye-free detergent. Wash new items before using them. Rinse baby laundry twice to remove traces of harsh chemicals.
- Avoid direct sun exposure to prevent sunburn.
- To prevent heat rash, don't let your baby get overheated.
- Clothe your baby in soft fabrics to avoid irritation.

To prevent or treat skin irritation in your baby's diaper area, try the following tips:

- Breastfeed. Stools from formula are more caustic.
- Change diapers often.
- Thoroughly clean your baby's bottom at each change. Avoid wipes that contain perfume or alcohol.

- Let your baby's bottom air-dry after cleaning it. Apply a barrier cream or jelly before rediapering. Avoid baby powder, which can encourage yeast growth.
- Use a mild, fragrance- and dye-free detergent to wash cloth diapers. Run an extra rinse cycle with 1/2 cup vinegar.
- Avoid moisture-trapping diaper covers made of vinyl, plastic, or rubber.
- If you use disposable diapers, choose a fragrance- and dye-free brand or one made of hypoallergenic materials.
- If your baby's bottom has a rash despite careful diapering and/or applications of over-the-counter diaper rash cream, consult your baby's caregiver.

During the first few months, your baby may develop any of the following skin conditions. These are all harmless and non-itching, and they eventually disappear without treatment.

- Newborn rash appears on the trunk, arms, and legs in the first week. It produces red blotches with yellow or white pimples in the middle. Many parents who have pets fear that these are fleabites. If you're concerned about fleas, put on clean white socks and shuffle through the house. If fleas are present, you'll see them on your socks.
- Facial rashes may consist of small red or white spots, rough red spots, red bumps, or smooth pimples.
- Cradle cap consists of scaly patches on the scalp and behind the ears.

Some newborn rashes, including cradle cap, are signs of an allergy. If your baby has a persistent, bothersome rash and you suspect an allergy, consult your baby's caregiver.

Cord Care

Your baby's umbilical cord stump will fall off within one to two weeks after birth. Before it falls off, it requires no special treatment. Simply let it dry naturally.

To help the cord stay dry and clean, wash your hands before touching it. Fasten diapers below the cord. If the cord gets dirty, wash it with plain warm water or gently dab it with alcohol on a cotton ball. Call your baby's caregiver if the cord grows red, smells bad, oozes pus, or bleeds.

Penis Care

An intact penis should be left alone. Do not retract (pull back) the foreskin for cleaning. A boy's foreskin doesn't retract fully until he is four to eight years old. Ordinary bathing is enough to keep the area clean.

If your newborn son is circumcised, healing takes seven to ten days. While the penis is healing, put a glob of jelly or barrier cream on a small square of gauze and gently place the gauze on the head of the penis. If your baby's caregiver left a small plastic ring on your son's penis, the ring (and foreskin) should fall off on its own in seven to ten days. Do not pull it off. Ask your baby's caregiver for bathing instructions during the healing period. Call your caregiver if the penis swells, bleeds, or oozes pus, or if your son doesn't urinate.

Notes:

Taking Temperature

Take your baby's temperature if you notice any of the following symptoms:

- Your baby is especially irritable.
- Your baby has a rash or is hot, sweaty, flushed, or pale.
- Your baby is breathing unusually fast, slow, or noisily.
- Your baby is sneezing, coughing, or has a runny nose.
- Your baby's appetite is poor.
- Your baby rubs his or her ears.
- Your baby is listless.
- Your baby has diarrhea or is vomiting.

The most accurate ways to check a newborn's temperature are rectally or in the armpit. To take a rectal temperature, use a digital rectal thermometer. Coat the thermometer bulb with petroleum or nonpetroleum jelly. Gently insert the thermometer no more than ½ inch (1.3 cm) into your baby's rectum. Hold the thermometer in place until it beeps.

To take an axillary (underarm) temperature, make sure your baby's armpit is dry. Place the bulb in your baby's armpit and hold that arm snugly against your baby's body. Wait until the thermometer beeps.

Remove the thermometer and read the temperature. Clean the thermometer with rubbing alcohol or with soap and cold water.

Consult your baby's caregiver if your baby's temperature is below 97.4°F (36.3°C) by either method. You should also call if your baby's axillary temperature exceeds 99.5°F (37.5°C) or your baby's rectal temperature exceeds 100.4°F (38°C).

Safety

Vehicles

Car accidents are the most common cause of infant death in the United States. In these accidents, no car safety seat is used, the car safety seat is improperly installed, or the baby is positioned incorrectly in the car safety seat.

In the United States and Canada, all babies traveling in motorized vehicles must ride in government-approved car safety seats. A baby should ride in the back seat of a vehicle in a rear-facing car safety seat until the baby is at least two years old or until he or she reaches the highest weight *or* height allowed by the car safety seat's manufacturer. If you cannot afford a car safety seat, notify your caregiver. He or she may be able to connect you with an organization that can provide a free car safety seat.

Some hospital or birth center staff will not discharge your baby if you don't have a car safety seat correctly installed in your vehicle. However, most hospital staff are not qualified to install car safety seats correctly. To avoid problems at discharge and to ensure your baby's safety, take a class on correct car safety seat installation. Your baby's life may depend on it.

If your baby is small or premature, he or she may need to travel in a special car bed. Hospital staff will help you assess your baby's needs and obtain a car bed if necessary.

Notes:

Sleeping

Although smoking during pregnancy is the top risk factor for sudden infant death syndrome (SIDS), safe sleeping is key to reducing your baby's risk of SIDS and smothering. Follow these tips for nighttime and naptime safety:

- During the first six months, your baby should always sleep within sight of a responsible adult—in your room when you're sleeping, and within sight when you're awake. Do not put your baby to sleep in another room, even with monitoring equipment.
- Choose a firm, clean, flat surface for your baby's sleep space. Remove thick quilts, comforters, pillows, bumpers, and any soft, loose bedding or other items. Make sure there's no gap between the mattress and headboard, railing, wall, or crib slats. If you use a crib, choose one approved for safety.
- Dress your baby in the same amount of clothing as you wear for sleep. Never swaddle your baby for sleep or naps. Swaddling and overheating are both risks for SIDS.
- Babies should always sleep faceup (on their backs). Do not use pillows or props to keep your baby in a faceup position.
- A person should not share a bed with a baby if:
  * The person has consumed anything that might cause drowsiness or hamper reflexes, such as alcohol or medication.
  * The person is a smoker.
  * The person is not the baby's biological mother.
  * The baby is formula-fed.
  * The sleep surface is not a safe one.
  There is no published risk of smothering for bed-sharing babies and mothers when the mother is breastfeeding and is a sober nonsmoker and when the sleep space is a safe one. Exclusively breastfed babies are the safest when bed sharing, and exclusively breastfeeding mothers who bed-share safely with their babies get the most rest.
- Never let your baby sleep on a couch or recliner, alone or with anybody else. The risk of smothering is very high.
- Have a fan circulating air where your baby sleeps.
- Let your baby suck on his or her fingers while sleeping.
- Formula-feeding parents may want to give their baby a pacifier for sleep after the first month. They should closely monitor their sleeping baby.

Shaking

Adjusting to parenthood can be stressful and exhausting. Normal infant crying can aggravate a parent's frustration. No matter how frustrated you get, **never shake your baby**. Shaking your baby can cause brain damage or death. If you feel tempted to shake your baby, place him or her in a safe space such as a crib or infant seat, walk away until you are calm, and ask another adult for help.

Feeding

Breastfeeding

The First Hour After Birth

Immediately after birth, your caregiver should place your baby directly on your chest, dry your baby, and place a warm towel over both of you. Even if your baby is born by cesarean, immediate and uninterrupted skin-to-skin contact helps you and your baby get off to a good start.

During the first hour, your baby will go through nine stages of adjustment to the world outside your body:

1. the birth cry, which expands your baby's lungs
2. relaxation
3. awakening
4. activity
5. rest
6. crawling toward your breast
7. getting familiar with your body and breast
8. suckling
9. sleeping contentedly on your chest

It's important to let your baby go through these stages at his or her own pace. This process is crucial to your baby's development. When your baby moves to your breast independently, the first nursing session is comfortable for both of you.

Positioning and Latch

For the best possible start at breastfeeding, take advantage of your newborn's initial alertness. Delay non-emergency medical procedures and other interruptions for the first hour, or until after the first good nursing session.

Snuggle your baby skin-to-skin on your chest, with a blanket over both of you. Eventually your baby will move his or her head about, looking and feeling for your nipple. Support your baby's neck, shoulders, and back, but don't hold your baby's head. When your baby finds your nipple, his or her mouth will open wide and latch on. Pull your baby close, letting his or her head tilt back a bit for easy swallowing.

Your baby can get into a good position for nursing if you set the stage and let your baby move to the breast independently. A reclining (semi-sitting) position is often better than sitting upright. Support your baby's body and head, but let your baby use his or her hands and body to move around your chest and get into position. Don't force your baby's head onto the breast. Doing so makes feedings harder for both of you.

Days One and Two

After your baby has moved to your breast and nursed, you both will probably sleep for a few hours—preferably touching one another on a safe bed. For the rest of the first day, your baby will nurse on and off all day and night, every couple of hours. Your baby may nurse eight to twelve times—or perhaps only six or seven times—in the first twenty-four hours.

Do not force feedings in the first twenty-four hours. Just keep your baby with you and feed whenever your baby shows hunger cues. Hungry babies are alert and active. They may put their hands in their mouths, make sucking motions, or turn their heads back and forth looking for the breast. Crying is a late sign of hunger.

Your newborn's stomach is very small, about the size of a marble or grape. During the first day, your baby learns to suck, swallow, and breathe in a smooth and coordinated manner. The small amount of colostrum your breasts make is perfectly suited to your baby's initial needs.

On day two, your baby will continue with a similar feeding pattern as your milk production increases. Expect your baby to nurse about every sixty to ninety minutes—for about ten to thirty minutes each time—on and off all day and night. Your baby will sleep an hour or so at a time. In these early days, don't expect your baby to go for long stretches without nursing or to sleep in long stretches.

Days Three through Five

Brace yourself for rapid and major changes in yourself and your baby on days three through five. These days are the most challenging for many mothers.

Your baby will continue feeding every sixty to ninety minutes and sleeping in sixty- to ninety-minute segments. Sleep and feeding patterns are usually irregular at this stage. Your baby may have one two- to four-hour sleep stretch each day, but longer stretches or multiple long stretches per day are rare. (See pages 112 and 119 for more information on sleep patterns and sleep safety.)

Your baby's stomach is growing bigger as your milk production increases. By the end of the first week, your baby's stomach is about the size of a walnut, and he or she takes up to 1 ounce (30 ml) of milk at each feeding. Trying to feed your baby larger amounts can cause a stomachache or vomiting. Spacing feeds further apart can cause intense pain from hunger. Small, frequent feeds are important for all babies.

Always let your baby finish the first breast first. Your baby will release your nipple or fall asleep when he or she is finished with the breast. Your baby may take both breasts or just one breast at a feeding. Some babies always take one breast per feed, some babies always take both breasts, and about half of babies vary their pattern throughout the day.

A feeding may be as short as seven minutes or as long as twenty-five minutes. If feedings are consistently shorter than ten minutes or longer than thirty minutes, or if they are painful or uncomfortable for you or your baby, *call a lactation consultant or other breastfeeding helper right away!*

Days Six through Fourteen

As the days pass, your baby's sleep and nursing patterns will probably become a little more predictable. By day five, each day your baby will be passing at least three to five loose yellow stools, wetting many diapers, and gaining a little weight. If you watch for signs of hunger or tiredness and respond promptly, your baby should be content most of the time.

Your breasts may not feel full most of the time. This is a good sign; it means that your breasts have adjusted, and your body is making milk in rhythm with your baby's needs. If, for whatever reason, your baby needs more milk on a given day, your baby will simply nurse more often and/or longer. An increase in nursing signals your body to make more milk.

Do not try to stretch the time between feeds, use a pacifier, give your milk in a bottle, or give formula supplements to make your baby sleep longer or nurse less. Those actions work against breastfeeding success.

Many babies seem to nurse more often around the end of the second week. This feeding increase could be due to a growth spurt. (All babies grow in spurts.)

Two to Six Weeks

Now you're getting into the swing of things. Breastfeeding should be comfortable and pleasant for both you and your baby. You might feel well enough and confident enough to take your baby on an errand or two. Take it easy, though—your body is still healing from birth.

Your baby is nursing between eight and sixteen times per twenty-four hours, day and night. You might see some new feeding and sleep patterns emerging. Your baby is having many bowel movements and wet diapers and is content most of the time. By six weeks, your milk production exceeds your baby's needs, and milk supply worries should be over.

Six Weeks to Four Months

Now the fun begins! Your baby is more alert now and may smile at you during nursing, reach for your face, and watch you intently. Your baby may be nursing as often as a newborn or might stretch out the time between some feeds. Your baby knows what he or she needs, and you are feeling more confident meeting those needs.

Most days have a comfortable rhythm. Your baby's sleep patterns might be more predictable. Sleeping together on a safe surface makes naps and night-times easy for both of you; you might not even fully wake for some feeds. (See page 119 for information on safe bed sharing.)

Four to Six Months and Beyond

In the past, many people thought that babies needed complementary foods (solid foods or family foods) by four months of age. But research now shows that your baby doesn't need anything except your milk for about six months—or possibly longer. Giving complementary foods before six months harms your baby's growth and increases the risk of illness.

When your baby is ready for complementary foods, he or she will show clear signs of readiness. Your baby will be able to sit upright without support. Your baby may reach for your plate or grab food off a table or tray. Your baby will be able to hold a piece of food, get it into his or her mouth, and chew (or gum) firm objects.

When your baby starts eating complementary foods, always breastfeed first. Then offer your baby nutritious foods that the rest of the family is eating. For more information, see the book *Baby-Led Weaning: The Essential Guide to Introducing Solid Foods and Helping Your Baby to Grow Up a Happy and Confident Eater* by Gill Rapley and Tracey Murkett.

During this phase, your baby may try to experiment with your breast by clamping down or biting. If this happens, promptly remove your baby from the breast. He or she will learn quickly that nursing and biting don't mix.

Even after your baby begins eating complementary foods, breastfeeding continues to provide immune protection and nutrition that your baby can't get anywhere else. You and your baby both benefit from breastfeeding for as long as you continue.

Eventually your baby will stop nursing when his or her needs are met. The World Health Organization (WHO) encourages mothers and babies around the world to continue breastfeeding (with family foods after six months) for two years or as long after that as they desire. No amount of time is "too long" for breastfeeding to continue.

What About Nursing in Public?

Most adults in the United States and elsewhere take the sight of a breastfeeding mother and baby in stride. Still, nursing in public is scary for many mothers. If you're afraid of what others may see during a feeding session, practice at home before going out, and go with other nursing mothers. If someone tells you "you can't breastfeed here," remember that most U.S. states—as well as most other countries—have laws to prevent people from harassing breastfeeding mothers.

Troubleshooting

Be patient with yourself and your baby while you're learning to breastfeed. You are both learning new skills. All new skills take practice. With practice and support, you and your baby will become an efficient breastfeeding team. Support has a strong effect on how long women breastfeed and how much women and their babies enjoy breastfeeding.

If you think your baby isn't getting enough milk, if your baby isn't feeding effectively, or if your nipples or breasts hurt, *see a breastfeeding helper today!* A challenge that seems impossible to you may be easily overcome by skilled helper, such as a lactation consultant, a La Leche League leader or peer counselor, a doula with breastfeeding training, your baby's caregiver, your caregiver, or an experienced mother. Most breastfeeding problems have fairly easy and comfortable solutions. Don't let modesty or feelings of inadequacy prevent you from asking for help or deprive you and your baby of breastfeeding's countless benefits.

If you hate breastfeeding, talk to your caregiver and a lactation specialist. They can help you sort out your feelings. Nobody wants to force mothers to do something they hate.

If you stopped breastfeeding and want to try again, call a lactation consultant right away. Relactation (restarting breastfeeding) is usually possible for at least six weeks after you stopped.

See page 30 for a list of online breastfeeding resources. For a comprehensive guide to breastfeeding, see the book *The Womanly Art of Breastfeeding* by La Leche League International.

Special Situations

If you and your baby are separated for an unavoidable reason—for example, if your baby is premature or sick or if you must return to work—and your baby can't nurse directly, your milk is still best for your baby. The next-best choice is donor milk from a certified milk bank. If your milk or donor milk is not available, a commercial formula is the only safe substitute.

Milk Collection and Storage

Hand-expressing milk is fairly easy, although it's a bit messy at first. Have a clean container with a wide mouth ready to collect the milk, and wash your hands. Position your breast over the container. Place your fingers and thumb on either side of your nipple, about 1 inch (2.5 cm) from the base of the nipple. Press straight back into your breast, then roll your fingers and thumb toward the nipple as you squeeze them together. Do not pinch the nipple or slide your fingers. (The motion is like squeezing ointment out of a tube.) Loosen your grip while leaving your fingers and thumb in the same positions. Then repeat the compression again and again in a rhythmic way. At first only a few drops will appear. Then your milk lets down, or starts flowing fast, and the milk sprays out each time you compress your breast. A milk letdown lasts about one to two minutes. Collect as much milk as you can before the letdown subsides. If you continue expressing, you'll feel another letdown in a few minutes. If you continue expressing until the second letdown subsides, you'll collect about 70 percent of the milk available in that breast. This is often 2 ounces (59 ml) or more per breast.

A good breast pump should be comfortable and easy to use with enough suction to collect milk. The flange, or the part that fits over your breast, should have a wide enough opening so your nipple moves easily inside it. If you use an electric pump with adjustable rhythm, start with a fast rhythm, then slow down a bit as the milk starts flowing. Pump through two letdowns plus another few minutes to get most of the available milk. Repeat in one to three hours. Wash your pump parts after each use. Be sure to read and follow the pump's use and care instructions.

You can store freshly collected milk in a clean container in the refrigerator for up to four days without losing any important nutrients or immune protection. Before using refrigerated milk, swirl it gently to mix the cream back into the milk. If you're not going to use the milk within a few days, freeze the milk in 1- to 3-ounce (30 to 89 ml) batches in freezer-safe containers. Thaw frozen milk carefully before using it. See http://www.cdc.gov/breastfeeding/recommendations/handling_breastmilk.htm for current milk storage and handling information.

Feeding Cups, Bottles, and Nipples

When your baby can't nurse directly, the next-best feeding method is using a small open cup. Unlike bottle-feeding, cup-feeding does not interfere with a nursing baby's sucking patterns and lets a baby control his or her intake of milk. Many babies who struggle with bottle-feeding—regardless of what's in the bottle—do well with cups.

At first, cup-feeding may seem awkward. It may feel time-consuming, or you may spill a little milk. But once you and your baby get the hang of cup-feeding, you'll find it easy and effective. To cup-feed your baby, follow these steps:

1. Pour a little milk into a small clean cup—about the size of a shot glass or a medicine cup.
2. Wrap your baby in a blanket to gently restrain his or her hands. Hold your baby in a semi-upright position, supporting his or her shoulders, neck, and head. Tuck a washcloth under your baby's chin.
3. Rest the rim of the cup on your baby's lower lip. Tilt the cup so the milk approaches your baby's lip, but do not pour the milk into your baby's mouth.
4. Let your baby smell the milk. Your baby will explore the milk with his or her tongue, then lap or sip the milk. Keep the cup at your baby's lip. Let your baby drink at his or her own pace, resting between sips. Refill the cup as needed.
5. Your baby will turn away when he or she is finished feeding.

Feeding bottles come in many sizes, shapes, and materials. Babies need small feeds, so use small 2- to 5-ounce (59 to 148 ml) bottles to avoid leftovers. A bottle's shape does not matter unless the shape makes the container hard to clean. Avoid bottles made with bisphenol-A (BPA), a chemical that may be harmful to children. Clean bottles with warm soapy water after every use, rinse them well, and let them air-dry.

Bottle nipples also come in many sizes, shapes, and flow rates. Despite advertising claims, no silicone or latex nipple is "closest to the breast." All artificial nipples are very different from mothers' breasts. The right nipple is one that lets your baby suck, swallow, and breathe comfortably at a pace similar to breast-feeding—about one suck, one swallow, and one breath per second. If milk flows too fast, your baby may struggle to breathe while feeding. If milk flows too slowly, your baby may get frustrated with having to work hard to feed. Test a few nipples to see which works best for your baby, and retest nipples every month or so. Clean nipples thoroughly with warm soapy water, rinse them well, and let them air-dry.

Some babies refuse to feed with a bottle and nipple. If your baby is one of them, go back to breastfeeding or try a small open cup instead.

Formula

Despite advertising claims, the nutritional differences among brands are small. Formulas made from cow's milk are generally better for babies than those made from soybeans. Formula provides adequate nutrition, but it does not provide any immune protection.

Notes:

Liquid ready-to-feed formula comes in sterile packaging and requires no added water. This type of formula is also the most expensive. Concentrated liquid formula also comes in sterile packaging, but it must be diluted with clean water according to the package instructions. **Avoid all liquid formula sold in metal cans; a toxic chemical called bisphenol A (BPA) can leach from the metal into the formula.**

Powdered formula is the least expensive type, but it is never sterile. It must be mixed with very hot water to minimize contamination risks. For both concentrated liquid formula and powdered formula, it's important to read labels and follow preparation directions carefully to avoid over- or under-concentration.

Warning Signs

Most babies stay healthy throughout the newborn period. But it's important to know the signs of a potential problem. If your baby shows any of the following symptoms during the first month, call his or her caregiver immediately. Your baby's caregiver can help you assess the situation and, if appropriate, begin treatment promptly.

- **Yellow skin or yellow whites of your baby's eyes** may be a sign of jaundice.
- **Less than one wet diaper for each day of age in the first week** may be a sign of undereating or illness.
- **Fewer than six wet diapers in one day after the first week** may be a sign of undereating or illness.
- **Dark yellow or orange urine** may be a sign of undereating.
- **No bowel movements in any twenty-four-hour period during the first month** may be a sign of undereating.
- **Very watery and frequent stools, possibly foul-smelling or containing mucus or blood**, may be a sign of diarrhea.
- **Any temperature below 97.4°F (36.3°C), axillary temperature above 99.5°F (37.5°C), or rectal temperature above 100.4°F (38°C)** may be a sign of infection.
- **Listlessness or unusual fussiness** may be a sign of illness, undereating, or diarrhea.
- **Umbilical redness, bleeding, oozing, or foul odor** may be a sign of umbilical infection.
- **Swollen, bleeding, or oozing penis or inability to urinate** may be a sign of infection or improper healing of circumcision.
- **Nursing fewer than eight times per twenty-four hours** may be a sign of illness or breastfeeding challenges.
- **Blue lips, flared nostrils, chest indentation, or trouble breathing** may be a sign of severe illness or respiratory problems. **CALL 911.**

Chapter 9
Dads and Partners

When a woman becomes pregnant, her partner embarks on the journey to parenthood with her. They have some similar experiences along the way, but some different ones, too. This chapter discusses the unique questions and challenges expectant fathers and partners face.

During Pregnancy

You may feel a mixture of joy and trepidation—and many other emotions—over your partner's pregnancy. What do the next several months hold in store for you? The following paragraphs discuss how to handle various personal concerns you may have, as well as how to support your partner and prepare for the birth.

The Announcement Phase

Think back to how you felt when you got the news of a positive pregnancy test. You may have been happy and very excited. On the other hand, you may have been stunned and overwhelmed by the news. Regardless of your initial reaction, you probably went through a short announcement phase. During this phase, you told friends and family about the pregnancy.

Evolving Emotions

After the announcement phase, some fathers and partners put away thoughts of the baby. Unless the mother is taking them to pick out paint colors for the nursery, they just don't think much about the baby.

During the first trimester, some fathers and partners constantly wonder about the health of the mother and baby. Your partner might be feeling tired and ill. Though you know these are common pregnancy discomforts, you may find it hard not to worry about her. And for at least a few months, you can't see any other evidence that she's pregnant. It's difficult to visualize your tiny, hidden baby and trust that all is well when no outward signs reassure you. Two simple strategies can calm your health worries and help you grasp your baby's existence.

1. **Read up.** Learn about the physical development occurring in your partner and baby. (See pages 2–5.) This will help you understand, visualize, and connect with what you can't see.
2. **Attend your partner's prenatal checkups.** At them you can ask questions, hear a heartbeat, and eventually see an ultrasound scan of your baby.

During the second trimester, many fathers and partners become very focused on their finances and jobs. If you find yourself doing this, it means you are dealing either consciously or subconsciously with financial changes looming on the horizon. Meanwhile, as your partner becomes more and more involved in her pregnancy, you may feel left out and out of touch with her. Sometime during the sixth month of pregnancy, you'll probably be able to feel the baby move through your partner's abdomen. This may help the baby seem more real to both of you. It may also help reconnect you and your partner.

During the third trimester, many fathers and partners become ready to begin learning about labor, birth, and the newborn. You might remain focused on your job, but now may also want to improve the family home, attend classes with your partner, and help with planning. By the end of pregnancy, you'll likely be as impatient for birth as your partner is.

Pregnancy may have a big—but largely unnoticed—impact on you throughout the experience. Your feelings toward your partner may run the gamut from passion to resentment, from loneliness to tenderness. Don't ignore your feelings. Sharing them with your partner can help you two reconnect. If relationship or family problems seem too knotty to resolve on your own, counseling may be helpful. Talking with an experienced friend or relative may also calm your mind.

Sexual Adjustments

When you become an expectant parent, the world shifts beneath your feet. You may feel uncertainty about your relationship with your partner. Your pregnant partner, naturally, is the focus of everyone's attention. She, in turn, may inadvertently focus her attention away from you. She may become introspective or reach out to experienced female friends and relatives.

During the first trimester of pregnancy, a mother may be less interested in sex than usual. Her body is producing many hormones that cause nausea and fatigue. Loss of interest in intercourse is common. Sex may need temporary replacement with hugs, kisses, massages, and snuggling.

During the second trimester, you may enjoy your partner's new figure. Your partner, in turn, may enjoy lovemaking more than ever. Her hormones may help her enjoy sex in a more intense way.

In the third trimester, women tend to feel big, hot, and tired of sharing their bodies. Lovemaking may drop on the priority list for a while. If this happens, be generous with compliments, hugs, kisses, and nonsexual romance.

Throughout pregnancy, you may wonder when sex is okay. It is okay whenever both of you agree and you have no medical reason to abstain. Sex is not okay if your partner's caregiver has told you to abstain, if your partner is at risk for preterm labor, if either of you has an infection, or if your partner's water has broken.

Many fathers and partners ask, "Will sex hurt the mother?" In a healthy pregnancy, sex is normal and safe. Let the mother control the position for maximum comfort. Hormonal changes may cause the vagina to feel dry and irritated, so use a water-soluble lubricant. If the mother complains of pain or bleeding, stop. She should share these concerns with her caregiver. The two of you may have to explore other ways to be intimate and stay close.

Another common concern among fathers and partners is whether sex will hurt the baby. Intercourse is safe for the baby in a healthy pregnancy. The baby is inside an amniotic sac, which cushions and protects the baby from the outside world.

Physical Symptoms

Some expectant fathers and partners feel physical discomforts. While your partner is pregnant, you may experience weight gain, difficulty sleeping, fatigue, food cravings, nausea, digestive problems, headaches, toothaches, dizziness, mood swings, or other pregnancy-like symptoms. These symptoms are called Couvade Syndrome, or sympathetic pregnancy. They are common, and they subside along with the mother's symptoms.

If your symptoms are bothersome or interfere with your ability to function normally, visit your caregiver. He or she may have ideas to help you reduce your anxiety and discomfort.

Supporting Your Partner

The more you can help your partner during pregnancy, the better off you both will be. You can support your partner emotionally and physically in several ways. Following are some suggestions.

Emotional Support

The key to supporting your partner emotionally is paying attention to her. Educate yourself about pregnancy and try to understand the ups and downs—emotional and physical— she's experiencing. Don't take mood swings personally. Show your interest in the pregnancy by attending prenatal exams and asking about test results. Encourage your partner. Ask her how she's feeling. If she's anxious,

upset, uncomfortable, or otherwise distressed, find out why and make an effort to alleviate the problem. Though you can't solve every problem your partner may have, your compassion and solidarity will sustain her.

Physical Support

If your partner is feeling exhausted, ill, or otherwise out of sorts, you can assist her with various comfort measures. (See pages 47–61.) You can also help her feel more comfortable by taking over any unpleasant, taxing, or risky household tasks.

For example, you can recruit a friend to help you with furniture moving, wall painting, and floor scrubbing to prepare for your baby's arrival. If your partner is usually the chef but now finds cooking nauseating, you can take over kitchen patrol. If your family already includes a child or children, you can assume a larger share of child-care responsibilities. If you have a pet—especially a cat—declare yourself the head poop-scooper. (Pregnant women should avoid cat feces. These may contain the toxoplasmosis parasite, which is dangerous to developing fetuses.)

In addition, you can help your partner have a healthy pregnancy by living a healthy lifestyle together. Make an effort to buy and prepare nutritious foods. Exercise regularly and sleep adequately. Avoid dangerous substances and activities. One of the most important things you can do to protect your family is to avoid smoking. Don't let anyone smoke around your family, in your car, or in your home. Finally, learn the warning signs of pregnancy complications (see page 14). If you observe any, encourage your partner to call her caregiver.

Preparing for Birth

Following are several important ways you and your partner can share the job of preparing for birth.

- **Choose maternity care together.** Your partner's caregiver and birthplace can strongly influence the type of birth that unfolds. Understand your insurance coverage and learn about the options available to you. Discuss preferences and options with your partner and choose maternity care that suits both of you. (See pages 16–20 for more information.)
- **Get educated.** Along with your partner, sign up for any pregnancy and parenting classes your community offers. Childbirth education should top your list. You might also take a breastfeeding class, a newborn-care class, infant CPR, or a course especially for fathers and partners. In addition, read up on

childbirth and newborn care. Ask friends and relatives with children for the straight scoop on daily life with a newborn.

- **Practice.** If you take a childbirth class with your partner, you'll learn many techniques for relaxation, coping with labor pain, and promoting labor progress. (See pages 47–61 for more information.) The more often you practice these techniques together, the more likely you'll remember, use, and benefit from them during your baby's birth.
- **Write a birth plan together.** Writing a birth plan will help you examine your feelings and beliefs about birth, discover and consider your options, clarify the role you'll play, and communicate your preferences clearly to your partner's caregiver and birthplace. (See Chapter 6 for more information.)
- **Think through labor logistics.** Answer the following questions with your partner: What needs to happen when labor begins? Who and what will you need with you? Who needs to know? Pack your birth bags or assemble your home birth supplies and put them in an accessible place. Line up transportation, child care, pet care, and other needs in advance.
- **Plan for postpartum together.** Discuss newborn-health decisions such as feeding, vaccination, circumcision, and cord blood collection. (See pages 26–34.) Recruit people to help you with basic household tasks during the first several weeks after birth. (See pages 39–40.) Decide parental leave and child-care arrangements, and take steps to implement them. (See pages 24–25.)

During Childbirth

Only your partner can birth your baby. But there's much you can do to support her during childbirth.

Labor Support

When labor begins, you may feel simultaneously excited and terrified. After the shock subsides, you can settle into your labor support role. The following describe key ways in which partners can support mothers in labor.

- During prelabor and early labor, join your partner in distracting activities. Try to be patient, cheerful, and attentive. Call your partner's caregiver and take care of any last-minute logistics.
- In active labor, help your partner with a variety of comfort measures, such as heat and cold, rhythmic breathing, relaxation exercises, massage, bathing or showering, acupressure, movement and positioning, and so on. (See pages 50–57 for more information.)
- At the beginning of each contraction, stop whatever you are doing and focus on your partner. Time her contractions. (See page 45.) Encourage her to rest between contractions.
- Stay near your partner and focus on her.
- Match your partner's mood and behavior. If she is quiet and focused, don't distract her. If she is talkative, then you and others may talk.
- Encourage and reassure your partner when she becomes frustrated or anxious. You can convey reassurance and encouragement with your body

Notes:

language by wearing a confident expression, speaking soothingly, and moving smoothly and slowly.

- Stay flexible and positive with both your partner and her caregiver. Encourage others in the room to stay positive or to leave the labor room.
- Help your partner care for her body by offering her food or drink, ice chips, or lip balm; by brushing her hair or washing her face; or by helping her use the bathroom.
- Communicate your partner's thoughts and desires to her caregiver and other staff.
- Supervise traffic in the labor room. Shoo out anyone who is not there to support your partner physically or emotionally.
- Take care of yourself so you can continue to support your partner. Eat and drink when you need to. Use good body mechanics and avoid overexerting yourself. Rest occasionally, either between contractions or when others offer to help.
- Help your partner during the pushing stage by physically supporting her through position changes. Encourage her to relax her perineum as she pushes. Cheer her on!

If you're worried that having a great deal of responsibility during labor will make it less enjoyable, discuss hiring a birth doula. A birth doula will not only meet your partner's physical and emotional needs, but will also give you the freedom to support your partner according to your own comfort level. See page 96 for more information about birth doulas.

Birth and Recovery

When your baby finally emerges, you'll probably feel a rush of emotions, including joy, relief, amazement, exhaustion, and affection. But at that moment your work isn't over; it's just beginning. The following are important ways you can support your partner and your newborn just after birth.

- Witness your baby's birth. If you wish and your partner's caregiver consents, catch your baby and cut the umbilical cord.
- For an hour or two, create a quiet, private space around your partner and baby. Delay interruptions and nonvital medical procedures. Snuggle with your partner as she holds your baby skin-to-skin. Talk quietly with your partner and your baby. Encourage your partner to breastfeed your baby during this brief alert period.
- If immediate skin-to-skin contact between your partner and your baby is impossible because of medical concerns for the baby, stay with your baby. Talk to your baby and report events to your partner.
- If immediate skin-to-skin contact between your partner and your baby is impossible because of medical concerns for your partner, consider holding your baby skin-to-skin yourself.
- If your baby is born at a hospital or birth center, stay overnight with your partner and baby.
- Be present for all newborn procedures.
- Take an active role in newborn care, such as diapering, bathing, dressing, swaddling, holding, and rocking.

Cesarean Birth

If your baby is born by cesarean, you may wonder how you can possibly be helpful. Here are some ideas.[1]

- Read pages 82–84 to understand the reasons for a cesarean and how the procedure unfolds.
- Once you, your partner, and her caregiver have agreed upon a cesarean, don't dwell on it. Focus on helping your partner and welcoming your baby as best you can. Remember that you still have an important role to play. It's just a different one.
- Before the surgery, ask who and what are permitted in the operating room. Can you be present? Can a second support person, such as a doula, be present? Can you take photos or video of the surgery?
- If you're worried about your reaction to watching surgery, ask the anesthesiologist for ideas to manage your anxiety.
- Sit at your partner's head so you can see and talk to each other. Focus on your partner as much as possible. Stay with her, ask questions, hold her hand, stroke her head, and report on what's happening. If she indicates pain or discomfort, alert her caregiver. If she wants you to take photos or video of the surgery, do so.
- If you want to see or photograph what's happening, or if your partner wants a progress report, stand at your partner's head and look over the sterile drape at the surgical site.
- If your partner feels anxious, help her use relaxation exercises or rhythmic breathing.
- If your partner needs to vomit, hold a basin for her.
- As soon as your baby emerges, be where your partner wants you to be. Chances are, she wants you to be with your baby. Tell your partner what's happening. Talk to your baby. Hold your baby and bring him or her to your partner as soon as you can.
- Help your partner begin breastfeeding soon—on the operating table or in the recovery room, if possible. If your partner is groggy, help her hold your baby during breastfeeding. If she has trouble latching your baby, ask a nurse, doula, or lactation consultant for help. Resist the urge to help your partner rest by feeding your baby with a bottle.
- Discuss the surgery afterward. Listen to your partner's experience and share what you remember. This discussion helps you fill in the blanks for each other.
- Understand that many women feel disappointed or conflicted after having a cesarean, regardless of the reason. Exercise patience and understanding during the postpartum period, as your partner comes to terms with her cesarean birth. Listen to her. Encourage her to seek professional help if she's having trouble coping with her feelings.

Notes:

Postpartum

Your baby is finally here, and your partner is recovering. And before you know it, you're on your own. When you're discharged from your birthplace or your home birth caregiver leaves, you may feel unready for the challenge of parenting. The following paragraphs offer strategies to help you adjust to postpartum life.

Addressing Personal Concerns

During the first weeks at home with your newborn, you may feel stretched thin. Your baby's needs are constant. Your partner is still recovering from birth, and she needs you, too. Don't forget about your own needs during this time. Taking care of yourself will help you take care of your family. Use the following tips to keep your personal reserves from running dry.

- **Get enough rest.** Work with your partner to share baby care and other duties, so each of you gets adequate time for resting and sleeping. Resist the urge to do too much. (See page 104 for more ideas to help you get enough rest.)
- **Eat nutritious foods.** You may be unable to enjoy a normal family meal for a while. But when you do eat, make it count. If you're well nourished, you'll feel better in both body and mind.
- **Exercise daily.** Even the simplest physical activity will brighten your outlook and boost your energy. At the least, take a daily walk with your baby in a carrier or stroller. A change of scenery and some fresh air will do you both good, and your partner will welcome the break.
- **Reach out.** Share your joys and frustrations with others, such as your partner, your parents and siblings, and your friends. Take a father–baby class or any class for new parents. You'll learn great ideas, find the humor in your struggles, and prevent feelings of isolation or inadequacy.

You may experience your own version of baby blues (see pages 106 and 135) due to sleep deprivation, new schedules, guilt if your partner seems overwhelmed, and being overwhelmed yourself. Talking to other fathers or parents can be very helpful. In addition, you can visit your local library or bookstore and check out a book that helps new fathers or parents adjust.

Supporting Your Partner

Your partner undergoes a dramatic adjustment during postpartum. She's not only recovering from childbirth, but also experiencing hormonal fluctuations, learning to breastfeed, and adjusting to life with a baby. You can support your partner physically and emotionally in several ways. In addition, you can hire a postpartum doula. These professionals are trained to provide emotional and physical support to families during postpartum. (See page 39 for more information.)

Physical Support

Your partner's body has performed an amazing feat. She has grown and birthed a baby, and if she's breastfeeding, she's now nourishing your baby with her body. It'll be several weeks before her body is fully recovered from childbirth and adjusted to mothering. During this time, she needs your help to avoid overexerting herself. Here are some ways you can support your partner physically:

- During the first week or two, help your partner avoid heavy lifting, stair climbing, or other strenuous activity by doing it for her.
- Your partner may spend a lot of time tethered to a chair, breastfeeding your newborn. She has little time or space to tend to her own physical needs. Make sure she has a steady supply of water and healthy snacks she can eat with one hand. When she's not nursing, take your baby so your partner can shower, use the bathroom, change clothes, exercise, or otherwise care for herself.
- Remember that your partner's perineum will be sore and healing for several weeks. In addition, hormonal changes and fatigue may dampen her libido. Talk respectfully with your partner about your sexual desires. Show affection in other ways if she's not yet ready for sex. When you resume sexual intercourse, take it slow and easy. Use a water-soluble lubricant if necessary. If you want to avoid another pregnancy, use contraception.
- Learn the warning signs of postpartum complications (see page 108). If you observe any, encourage your partner to call her caregiver.

Emotional Support

The key to supporting your partner emotionally during postpartum, just as during pregnancy, is paying attention to her. Ask her how she's doing. Ask her what she needs. Listen to her replies, and meet her emotional needs to the best of your ability. Understand that she doesn't expect you to fix everything, but to listen with empathy.

Be aware that many women feel sad, upset, or anxious after giving birth. This condition, called baby blues, is a normal result of hormonal changes plus the stress of parenting a newborn. (See page 106 for more information.) You can help your partner overcome baby blues by making it possible for her to get enough rest, encouraging her to control any pain she's having, and being available to support her.

If your partner's sadness lasts more than two weeks or begins after two weeks, she may be developing a more serious emotional disorder. (See pages 106–107 to learn about postpartum mood disorders and postpartum psychosis.) If your partner shows signs of these disorders, call her caregiver for advice.

Sharing the Load

You may be surprised at how much time, energy, and patience it takes to meet the needs of a tiny baby. Caring for a newborn is hard work, even for experienced parents. As you face this challenge together, recognize that it's stressful for both of you. You can lighten the load by sharing parenting and household duties and by giving your relationship the attention it needs.

Parenting Duties

Because your partner carried your baby for nine months, your baby is accustomed to her sounds, smells, and motions. She may find it easier to soothe your baby than you do. And if she's breastfeeding, she's got one important baby-care

Notes:

tool that you don't have. But there's still plenty you can do to share in parenting. Here are some ideas. (See Chapter 8 for more information on newborn care.)

- Bring your baby to your partner for nursing.
- Burp your baby after feedings.
- Change your baby's diaper.
- Cuddle your baby and rock him or her to sleep.
- Spend time with your baby. Walk, play, dance, and talk with your baby. Sing and read to your baby.
- Hold your baby often, especially when he or she fusses or cries. Remember that you cannot spoil a baby.
- If your partner is pumping breast milk, or if your baby is formula-fed, feed your baby with a cup or bottle.
- Be present for well-child visits.
- Give older children the time and attention they need every day. Take your baby so your partner can focus on your older children, too.

Household Duties

Household management is an area in which you can be very useful after your baby's birth. When you take charge of household needs, you make it easier for your partner to recover and to adjust to the responsibilities of motherhood. Following are key ways you can shoulder the household load:

- Keep the refrigerator and cupboards well supplied with healthy, easy-to-prepare foods.
- Assume chef duty. If you can't cook, or if your partner enjoys cooking, take the baby so she can spend some time in the kitchen.
- If you have pets, make sure they get the proper amount of food, water, exercise, and attention. Clean up after them.
- Tidy up when you can. Pick up clutter as you notice it. Toss in a load of laundry when you think of it. Do the dishes. Make the bed. Sweep the floor. Wipe the countertop. Change the toilet paper roll. Little efforts add up.
- Accept, recruit, and organize household help and meals from friends, relatives, neighbors, coworkers, and so on.
- Manage visitors to suit your family's needs. If it's been a taxing day, politely decline visitors so your family can rest. Invite them over later, when you're feeling more sociable and energetic.

Your Relationship

During pregnancy, you may have had sweet dreams of family life after your baby's birth. Don't be alarmed if the reality is occasionally less than dreamy.

Newborns are disruptive. They change comfortable routines, causing confusion until everyone in the family settles into new patterns. They demand constant attention, drawing focus away from other relationships.

Supporting each other in your new roles can go a long way toward preserving a happy, healthy relationship. So can setting aside time to focus on each other and nurture shared interests.

If either partner feels unsupported, or if you and your partner feel your daily lives growing in different directions after your baby's birth, your relationship may suffer. You may also struggle to stay connected if your partner or your baby has health problems.

If you think your relationship is falling apart, you'll both need to participate in its repair. Discuss the issues as calmly as possible. Seek counseling to learn practical strategies for strengthening your bond and parenting as partners.

Conclusion

Your journey to parenthood is a pivotal life experience. It can also be a wild ride—exciting, empowering, and overwhelming all at once. As you enjoy the surprises and pleasures along the way, you also face new responsibilities and a variety of physical and emotional challenges.

By educating yourself about pregnancy, birth, and parenting, you help your confidence grow. You strengthen your relationship with your partner, with your family and friends, and with your caregiver and community. You increase the joys of your journey while navigating its challenges more easily.

Remember that only you and your partner can make the best choices for your family. Armed with solid information from this book, from your caregiver, and from other trustworthy resources, you'll be well equipped to handle any decisions that come along.

Have faith in yourselves. And enjoy the ride!

Notes

Chapter 1: Pregnancy

1. Fetal Development, "Week Thirty Seven: Pregnancy is considered 'at term'," 2011, http://www.baby2See.com/development/week37.html (May 1, 2011).
2. "March of Dimes Praises New ACOG Guidelines on the Induction of Labor," March of Dimes, August 2009, http://www.marchofdimes.com/news/aug_2009.html (May 1, 2011).
3. See note 1.
4. See note 2.
5. Penny Simkin, Janet Whalley, Ann Keppler, Janelle Durham, and April Bolding, *Pregnancy, Childbirth, and the Newborn* (Minneapolis, MN: Meadowbrook Press, 2010), 110.
6. CDA Foundation, "Oral Health during Pregnancy and Early Childhood: Evidence-Based Guidelines for Health Professionals," *Perinatal Oral Health*, February 2010, http://www.cdafoundation.org/library/docs/poh_guidelines.pdf (April 15, 2010).
7. March of Dimes, "Caffeine in Pregnancy," *March of Dimes: Medical References*, February 2008, http://www.marchofdimes.com/professionals/14332_1148.asp (April 19, 2010).
8. Marc Tunzi and Gary R. Gray, "Common Skin Conditions During Pregnancy," *American Family Physician*, January 15, 2007, 211–218.
9. A. L. Coker, M. Sanderson, and B. Dong, "Partner Violence during Pregnancy and Risk of Adverse Pregnancy Outcomes," *Paediatric and Perinatal Epidemiology*, July 2004, 260–269.
10. Childbirth Connection, "Needs of Healthy Childbearing Women," *Childbirth Connection: Vision, Mission, and Beliefs*, February 28, 2006, https://www.childbirthconnection.org/article.asp?ck=10175&ClickedLink=539&area=3 (April 21, 2010).
11. Penny Simkin, Janet Whalley, Ann Keppler, Janelle Durham, and April Bolding, *Pregnancy, Childbirth, and the Newborn* (Minneapolis, MN: Meadowbrook Press, 2010), 70.

Chapter 3: Preparing for Baby

1. American Academy of Family Physicians, "Circumcision," *FamilyDoctor.org*, May 2009, http://familydoctor.org/online/famdocen/home/men/reproductive/042.html (July 1, 2010).
2. World Health Organization and Joint United Nations Programme on HIV/AIDS, "Male Circumcision: Global Trends and Determinants of Prevalence, Safety, and Acceptability," *World Health Organization*, 2007, http://whqlibdoc.who.int/publications/2007/9789241596169_eng.pdf (July 1, 2010).
3. Canadian Paediatric Society, "Circumcision: Information for Parents," *Caring for Kids*, November 2004, http://www.cps.ca/caringforkids/pregnancy&babies/circumcision.htm (July 1, 2010).
4. The Humane Society of the United States, "Introducing Your Pet and New Baby," *The Humane Society of the United States*, November 4, 2009, http://www.humanesociety.org/animals/resources/tips/pets_babies.html (July 2, 2010).
5. DONA International, "How to Hire a Doula," *DONA International*, n.d., http://www.dona.org/mothers/how_to_hire_a_doula.php (July 2, 2010).

Chapter 4: Childbirth Stages and Strategies

1. Wiley-Blackwell, "Eating and Drinking During Labor: Let Women Decide, Review Suggests," *ScienceDaily*, January 22, 2010, http://www.sciencedaily.com /releases/2010/01/100119213043.htm (May 10, 2010).
2. Elizabeth R. Cluett and Ethel Burns, "Immersion in Water in Labour and Birth," *Cochrane Database of Systematic Reviews*, 2009, http://mrw.interscience.wiley.com/cochrane/clsysrev/articles/CD000111/frame.html (May 12, 2010).
3. Hyangsook Lee and Edzard Ernst. "Acupuncture for Labor Pain Management: A Systematic Review. *American Journal of Obstetrics and Gynecology*, November 2004, http://www.ajog.org/article/S0002-9378(04)00510-1/abstract (May 14, 2010); Caroline A. Smith, Carmel T. Collins, Allan M. Cyna, and Caroline A. Crowther, "Complementary and Alternative Therapies for Pain Management in Labour," *Cochrane Database of Systematic Reviews*, 2009, http://mrw.interscience.wiley.com/cochrane/clsysrev/articles/CD003521/frame.html (May 14, 2010).
4. Christopher Lloyd Clarke, "Rapid Relaxation Script," *The Guided Meditation Site*, n.d., http://www.the-guided-meditation-site.com/rapid-relaxation-script.html (May 17, 2010).
5. Elizabeth R. Cluett and Ethel Burns, "Immersion in Water in Labour and Birth," *Cochrane Database of Systematic Reviews*, 2009, http://mrw.interscience.wiley.com/cochrane/clsysrev/articles/CD000111/frame.html (May 25, 2010).
6. Midwives Information and Resource Service, "The Use of Water in Childbirth," *MIDIRS*, 2007, http://data.memberclicks.com/site/wi/MIDIRS%20Waterbirth.pdf (May 25, 2010).
7. Marty O. Visscher, Vivek Narendran, William L. Pickens, Angela A. LaRuffa, Jareen Meinzen-Derr, Kathleen Allen, and Steven B. Hoath, "Vernix Caseosa in Neonatal Adaptation," *Journal of Perinatology*, April 14, 2005, http://www.nature.com/jp/journal/v25/n7/full/7211305a.html (May 26, 2010).
8. Henry T. Akinbi, Vivek Narendran, Amy Kun Pass, Philipp Markart, and Steven B. Hoath, "Host Defense Proteins in Vernix Caseosa and Amniotic Fluid," American *Journal of Obstetrics and Gynecology*, December 2004, http://www.ajog.org/article/S0002-9378(04)00466-1/abstract (May 26, 2010).

Chapter 5: Complications and Interventions

1. March of Dimes, "Group B Strep Infection," *March of Dimes*, March 2010, http://www.marchofdimes.com/professionals/14332_1205.asp (September 13, 2010).
2. Penny Simkin, Janet Whalley, Ann Keppler, Janelle Durham, and April Bolding, *Pregnancy, Childbirth, and the Newborn* (Minneapolis, MN: Meadowbrook Press, 2010), 131.
3. D. Simmons, "Epidemiologic context of diabetes in pregnancy." *A Practical Manual of Diabetes in Pregnancy* (Hoboken, NJ: Wiley-Blackwell, 2010).
4. American Diabetes Association, "Standards of Medical Care in Diabetes, *Diabetes Care* 2008; 31 (Supple 1): S12-S54
5. Preeclampsia Foundation, "About Preeclampsia," *Preeclampsia Foundation*, July 19, 2008, http://www.preeclampsia.org/about.asp (June 8, 2010).
6. M. Rabi, R. Ahner, M. Bitschnau, H. Zeisler, and P. Husslein, "Acupuncture for Cervical Ripening and Induction of Labor at Term—A Randomized Controlled Trial," *Wien Klin Wochenschr*, 2001, http://www.ncbi.nlm.nih.gov/pubmed/11802511?dopt=Abstract (June 11, 2010).

7. "March of Dimes Praises New ACOG Guidelines on the Induction of Labor," March of Dimes, August 2009, http://www.marchofdimes.com/news/aug_2009.html (May 1, 2011).

8. Ibid.

9. Josie L. Tenore, "Methods for Cervical Ripening and Induction of Labor," *American Family Physician*, May 15, 2003, http://www.aafp.org/afp/2003/0515/p2123.html (June 13, 2010).

10. Josie L. Tenore, "Methods for Cervical Ripening and Induction of Labor," *American Family Physician*, May 15, 2003, http://www.aafp.org/afp/2003/0515/p2123.html (June 13, 2010).

11. Josie L. Tenore, "Methods for Cervical Ripening and Induction of Labor," *American Family Physician*, May 15, 2003, http://www.aafp.org/afp/2003/0515/p2123.html (June 13, 2010); Penny Simkin, Janet Whalley, Ann Keppler, Janelle Durham, and April Bolding, *Pregnancy, Childbirth, and the Newborn* (Minneapolis, MN: Meadowbrook Press, 2010), 280.

12. Josie L. Tenore, "Methods for Cervical Ripening and Induction of Labor," *American Family Physician*, May 15, 2003, http://www.aafp.org/afp/2003/0515/p2123.html (June 13, 2010); Penny Simkin, Janet Whalley, Ann Keppler, Janelle Durham, and April Bolding, *Pregnancy, Childbirth, and the Newborn* (Minneapolis, MN: Meadowbrook Press, 2010), 280–282.

13. Carol Sakala and Maureen P. Corry, "Evidence-Based Maternity Care: What It Is and What It Can Achieve," *International Childbirth Education Association*, 2008, http://www.icea.org/sites/default/files/evidence-based-maternity-care.pdf (May 21, 2010).

14. Carol Sakala and Maureen P. Corry, "Evidence-Based Maternity Care: What It Is and What It Can Achieve," *International Childbirth Education Association*, 2008, http://www.icea.org/sites/default/files/evidence-based-maternity-care.pdf (May 21, 2010).

15. Penny Simkin, Janet Whalley, Ann Keppler, Janelle Durham, and April Bolding, *Pregnancy, Childbirth, and the Newborn* (Minneapolis, MN: Meadowbrook Press, 2010), 197; Childbirth Connection, "Narcotics," *Childbirth Connection: Labor Pain*, June 8, 2006, http://www.childbirthconnection.org/article.asp?ck=10189 (May 21, 2010).

16. Carol Sakala and Maureen P. Corry, "Evidence-Based Maternity Care: What It Is and What It Can Achieve," *International Childbirth Education Association*, 2008, http://www.icea.org/sites/default/files/evidence-based-maternity-care.pdf (June 14, 2010).

17. Murray Enkin, Marc J. N. C. Keirse, James Neilson, Caroline Crowther, Lelia Duley, Ellen Hodnett, and Justus Hofmeyr, *A Guide to Effective Care in Pregnancy and Childbirth* (New York: Oxford University Press, 2000), 397–403.

18. J. S. Read and M. L. Newell, "Efficacy and Safety of Cesarean Delivery for Prevention of Mother-to-Child Transmission of HIV-1," *Cochrane Database of Systematic Reviews*, October 19, 2005, http://www2.cochrane.org/reviews/en/ab005479.html (June 15, 2010).

19. Kevin S. Toppenberg and William A. Block, "Uterine Rupture: What Family Physicians Need to Know," *American Family Physician*, September 1, 2002, http://www.aafp.org/afp/2002/0901/p823.html (June 15, 2010).

20. Gerard G. Nahum and Krystle Quynh Pham, "Uterine Rupture in Pregnancy," E-*Medicine.Medscape*, May 12, 2010, http://emedicine.medscape.com/article/275854-overview (June 16, 2010).

21. Penny Simkin, Janet Whalley, Ann Keppler, Janelle Durham, and April Bolding, *Pregnancy, Childbirth, and the Newborn* (Minneapolis, MN: Meadowbrook Press, 2010), 280–282.

22. Eva Jungmann, "Caesarean Delivery to Prevent Neonatal Herpes," Clinical Evidence, April 1, 2007, http//clinicalevidence.bmj.com/ceweb/conditions/seh/1603/1603_I6.jsp (June 16, 2010).

23. Childbirth Connection, "Preventing Pelvic Floor Dysfunction," *Childbirth Connection: Preventing Pelvic Floor Dysfunction*, March 2, 2006, http://www.childbirthconnection.org/article.asp?ClickedLink=281&ck=10206&area=27 (June 16, 2010); Childbirth Connection, "Effect of Elective C-section," *Childbirth Connection: Preventing Pelvic Floor Dysfunction*, February 21, 2006, http://www.childbirthconnection.org/article.asp?ck=10200&ClickedLink=282&area=27 (June 16, 2010).

24. Saju Joy and Stephen A. Contag, "Cesarean Delivery: Treatment," E-*Medicine.Medscape*, May 28, 2010, http://emedicine.medscape.com/article/263424-treatment (June 17, 2010); Penny Simkin, Janet Whalley, Ann Keppler, Janelle Durham, and April Bolding, *Pregnancy, Childbirth, and the Newborn* (Minneapolis, MN: Meadowbrook Press, 2010), 314–317.

25. Childbirth Connection, "What Every Pregnant Woman Needs to Know about Cesarean Section," *Childbirth Connection*, December 2006, http://www.childbirthconnection.org/pdfs/cesareanbooklet.pdf (June 17, 2010).

26. Childbirth Connection, "What Every Pregnant Woman Needs to Know about Cesarean Section," *Childbirth Connection*, December 2006, http://www.childbirthconnection.org/pdfs/cesareanbooklet.pdf (June 18, 2010).

Chapter 6: Preparing for Birth

1. Carol Sakala and Maureen P. Corry, "Evidence-Based Maternity Care: What It Is and What It Can Achieve," *International Childbirth Education Association*, 2008, http://www.icea.org/sites/default/files/evidence-based-maternity-care.pdf (June 22, 2010).

2. DONA International, "How to Hire a Doula," *DONA International*, n.d., http://www.dona.org/mothers/how_to_hire_a_doula.php (June 23, 2010).

Chapter 7: Postpartum

1. Gordon Parker, Neville A. Gibson, Heather Brotchie, Gabriella Heruc, Anne-Marie Rees, and Dusan Hadzi-Pavlovic, "Omega-3 Fatty Acids and Mood Disorders," *The American Journal of Psychiatry*, June 2006, http://ajp.psychiatryonline.org/cgi/content/full/163/6/969 (September 15, 2010); Pamela K. Murphy and Carol L. Wagner, "Vitamin D and Mood Disorders Among Women: An Integrative Review: Overview of Vitamin D and Its Effects on Disease Processes," *Medscape*, 2008, http://www.medscape.com/viewarticle/579946_5 (September 15, 2010).

Chapter 8: Newborn Care

1. American Speech-Language-Hearing Association, "Hearing Loss," *American Speech-Language-Hearing Association*, n.d., http://www.asha.org/public/hearing/testing/ (July 14, 2010).

2. Kelly Bonyata, "Studies on Normal Infant Sleep," *Kellymom: Breastfeeding and Parenting*, April 5, 2010, http://www.kellymom.com/parenting/sleep/sleepstudies.html (September 15, 2010).

3. Janet Bryanton, Donna Walsh, Margaret Barrett, and Darlene Gaudet, "Tub Bathing Versus Traditional Sponge Bathing for the Newborn," *Journal of Obstetric, Gynecologic, and Neonatal Nursing*, March 9, 2006, http://www3.interscience.wiley.com/journal/118783692/abstract (July 16, 2010).

Chapter 9: Dads and Partners

1. Penny Simkin, *The Birth Partner*, 2nd edition (Boston: Harvard Common Press, 2001), 257–263.

Glossary

active labor	The middle phase of the first stage of labor. Active labor begins when the cervix dilates to 4 or 5 centimeters and ends when the cervix dilates to about 8 cm.
acupressure	The practice of pressing on specific points on the body to cure disease or relieve pain.
acupuncture	The practice of inserting fine needles through the skin at specific points on the body to cure disease or relieve pain.
afterpains	Uterine cramping and discomfort felt for a week or so after birth, as the uterus contracts and returns to its normal size.
amniohook	A device resembling a large crochet hook, inserted through the cervix and into the uterus to artificially rupture the amniotic sac.
amniotic fluid	A clear liquid surrounding a developing fetus inside the amniotic sac. Amniotic fluid protects the baby and provides fluids. The baby swallows this fluid and inhales it into his or her lungs. Amniotic fluid helps the lungs and digestive system develop and allows the baby to move around and develop his or her muscles and bones.
amniotic sac	A thin membrane containing a developing fetus and amniotic fluid.
amniotomy	Artificial rupture of the amniotic sac, also called artificial rupture of membranes (AROM).
analgesic	A drug that acts on the brain so the user doesn't recognize pain impulses.
anemia	Depleted iron stores in the body.
anesthetic	A drug that blocks nerves from sending pain impulses to the brain.
antibodies	Proteins that fight attacking microbes.
Apgar score	The result of a newborn assessment performed within one minute after birth and again at five minutes after birth. A caregiver evaluates the baby's muscle tone, heart rate, reflexes, skin color, and breathing, giving the baby a score from zero to two in each category. The sum of these scores is the baby's Apgar score.
auscultation	In labor, listening to the baby's heart rate intermittently before a contraction, during a contraction, and after a contraction.
baby blues	A common, mild, and temporary condition that usually begins between the third and fifth days postpartum. Symptoms include crying easily, occasional sadness, difficulty sleeping, irritability, mild anxiety, tiredness, difficulty concentrating, feeling overwhelmed or out of control, and low self-confidence.
bilirubin	A substance created when red blood cells break down.
birth certificate	An official document that records the birth of a child at a specific time, in a specific place, to a specific parent or set of parents.
birth doula	A professional trained in and experienced at supporting women and their partners during childbirth.
birth plan	A brief verbal or written statement that describes an expectant mother's preferences for care during childbirth and early postpartum.
bloody show	Loss of mucous plug in late pregnancy. The plug typically passes out of the vagina as thin, stringy mucus tinged with blood.
Braxton-Hicks contractions	Relatively painless, irregular "practice" contractions of the uterus that occur during pregnancy and increase over time but are not associated with labor.
breech presentation	A fetal posture in which one foot or both feet lie over the cervix. Frank breech is a fetal posture in which the buttocks lie over the cervix. Complete breech is a fetal posture in which the buttocks and feet lie over the cervix.
certified nurse-midwife (CNM)	A registered nurse with one or more years of additional training in midwifery. CNMs focus on the needs of healthy women during the childbearing year.
certified professional midwife (CPM)	A maternity caregiver with midwifery education, training, and apprenticeship who has passed an exam given by the North American Registry of Midwives (NARM). CPMs focus on the needs of healthy women during the childbearing year.
cervical position	Direction in which cervix is pointing, expressed as posterior, midline, or anterior.
cervix	The neck-like opening that lies at the lower end of the uterus and opens into the vagina.
cesarean birth	A type of surgery in which a caregiver cuts incisions in a pregnant woman's abdomen and uterus and lifts the baby out by hand.
chloasma	A darkening of skin around the eyes caused by pregnancy hormones, also called mask of pregnancy.
chorionic villi	In early pregnancy, a primitive placenta that allows the transfer of blood and nutrients from mother to fetus.
circumcision	The surgical removal of the foreskin, a layer of skin covering the glans (head) of the penis.
colostrum	A yellowish, highly nutritious first milk made by a mother's breasts during the first one to three days after giving birth.

complementary foods	Family foods, also called solid foods.
constipation	A condition in which the body produces hard, dry stools that are difficult to pass.
contraction	The shortening and thickening of a muscle. In labor, uterine contractions ripen, efface, and dilate the cervix. They also rotate and push the baby down and out of the uterus.
cord blood	The blood left inside the umbilical cord and placenta after the cord is cut following a baby's birth.
cord prolapse	Cord-first birth.
Couvade Syndrome	Pregnancy-like symptoms experienced by a pregnant woman's partner, also called sympathetic pregnancy.
delayed pushing	A method used when a laboring woman has had epidural or spinal anesthesia. She avoids pushing until her baby crowns or until she feels an urge to push.
descent	A process in which the baby moves lower into the mother's pelvis during late pregnancy or labor, also called lightening, dropping, or engagement.
diarrhea	A condition in which the body produces excessive watery stools.
dilation	Opening of cervix, measured in centimeters, with 10 cm indicating complete dilation.
dilator	A device that puts pressure on the inside of the cervix, which encourages the cervix to ripen, efface, and dilate.
directed pushing	A pushing method in which the mother bears down when told to do so.
Doptone	A handheld device that converts ultrasound readings of the fetal heartbeat into sounds.
early labor	The initial phase of the first stage of labor. Early labor starts with progressing contractions and lasts until the cervix dilates to 4 or 5 centimeters.
eclampsia	A life-threatening condition related to high blood pressure in pregnancy and developing from preeclampsia. Eclampsia is characterized by seizures, stroke, and/or coma.
ectopic pregnancy	Pregnancy in which the fertilized egg has implanted outside the uterus.
effacement	Thinning or shortening of the cervix, changing gradually from a turtleneck shape to crewneck shape, measured in percentages (100 percent indicating complete effacement) or centimeters (indicating the cervical length).
electronic fetal monitoring (EFM)	The use of two electronic sensors to detect contractions and fetal heart rate.
elimination communication (EC)	A diaper-free method of managing a baby's urine and stool output.
embryo	In human pregnancy, a developing baby from conception until about ten weeks LMP.
energy medicine	A group of therapies proposing that imbalances in an energy field surrounding and permeating the human body can cause illness and discomfort and that restoring balance can restore health and comfort.
engorgement	Painful swelling of the breasts during milk production.
epidural catheter	A method of delivering medication into the lower back, near nerve roots in the spine. A caregiver inserts a needle into the epidural space in the spine, threads a catheter through the needle, removes the needle, tapes the catheter to the back, and attaches the catheter to a device that steadily releases small amounts of medication.
episiotomy	A surgical incision to enlarge the vaginal opening.
express	In lactating women, to extract or pump milk from the breasts.
external version	A procedure in which a caregiver manipulates the outside of a pregnant woman's belly to try to turn a breech or transverse baby vertex.
failure to progress	A childbirth situation in which either dilation or pushing is taking longer than expected; in some cases called cephalo-pelvic disproportion (CPD).
family doctor	A doctor who has additional training in family medicine, including maternity care and pediatrics. Family doctors focus on the health care needs of the entire family.
fetoscope	A type of stethoscope used for listening to the fetal heartbeat.
fetus	In human pregnancy, a developing baby from eleven weeks LMP to birth.
first stage of labor	The part of labor that begins with progressing contractions and ends when the cervix is completely dilated. The first stage of labor includes early labor, active labor, and transition.
forceps	Long steel tongs used during childbirth to help the baby exit the mother's body.
gestational diabetes	A pregnancy condition in which the mother's body has trouble converting food into energy.
groin	Lower abdomen.

Group B streptococcus (GBS)	A bacterium carried by about 25 percent of women, usually in the vagina or rectum, that may pass to a baby during childbirth. GBS is usually harmless to adults but can cause serious illness in newborns.
guided imagery	A technique in which one concentrates on a series of mental images in order to relax and improve confidence.
HELLP syndrome	A life-threatening condition characterized by hemolysis, elevated liver enzymes, and low platelet count in the blood.
hemorrhage	Heavy bleeding.
hemorrhoids	Varicose veins in the rectum or anus.
hepatitis B	An infection of the liver caused by a blood-borne virus.
homeopathy	A type of medical care that treats a disease or condition by administering tiny doses of a remedy that would produce symptoms of the disease or condition in a healthy person. Homeopathic remedies are extracts of natural substances highly diluted in alcohol or water.
hydrotherapy	Water therapy.
hysterectomy	Surgical removal of the uterus.
informed decision-making	The ability to make decisions with access to all relevant information, including the best available research evidence on the benefits and risks of a treatment and its alternatives as well as caregiver guidance. An informed decision is based not only on the information and guidance received, but also on personal values and circumstances.
instrument delivery	In childbirth, using a vacuum extractor or forceps to help the baby exit the mother's body.
intact penis	Penis in its natural state, not circumcised.
intrauterine growth restriction	A condition in which a fetus has stopped growing and thriving inside the mother's body.
intravenous (IV)	Delivered directly into a person's vein.
involution	A postpartum process in which the uterus returns to its normal size. Involution begins as soon as a mother has expelled the placenta.
jaundice	A buildup of bilirubin in the blood.
Kegel exercises	A method of strengthening the pelvic floor muscles. A woman holds her breath, tightens her pelvic muscles as if stopping the flow of urine, holds this muscle contraction for ten seconds, and repeats the process several times.
labor induction	Attempting to start labor before it starts on its own.
lactation	Milk production.
lanugo	Downy hair covering a fetus's body.
letdown	A milk-ejection reflex that occurs in lactating women.
licensed midwife (LM)	A maternity caregiver who has completed the midwifery educational and apprenticeship requirements of her state and has passed an exam given by the state licensing board. LMs focus on the needs of healthy women during the childbearing year.
linea nigra	A dark line between the navel and pubic bone, caused by pregnancy hormones.
lochia	A vaginal discharge that begins immediately after childbirth and lasts four to six weeks. It contains blood, mucus, the tissue that lined the uterus during pregnancy, and various fluids.
macrosomia	In pregnancy, a very large baby.
maternity care	Health care given to the mother during pregnancy, labor and delivery, and recovery, and to the baby after birth.
mature milk	Whitish milk produced by a lactating woman starting between the second and fifth days postpartum.
meconium	Sticky, greenish-black stool passed by a newborn on the first day.
meditation	Deep concentration on a sound, object, image, movement, idea, or one's breathing.
membrane stripping or sweeping	A procedure in which a caregiver inserts a finger through the cervix and sweeps in a circular motion to detach the lower part of the amniotic sac from the inside of the uterus. This procedure stimulates prostaglandin release and also mechanically dilates the cervix.
microbes	Microscopic organisms such as bacteria, viruses, and parasites.
moxibustion	The placement of burning herbs close to acupuncture points.
mucous plug	Thick mucus that fills the opening of the cervix during pregnancy, sealing the uterus shut and protecting the baby from infection.
narcotic	A type of analgesic medication.
neonatal intensive care unit (NICU)	A protected environment designed for close observation and specialized medical care of sick or premature babies.

nesting	A late-pregnancy burst of energy.
nonprogressing contractions	Contractions that occur without changing in strength, length, or frequency. Nonprogressing contractions promote blood circulation in the uterus, press the baby against the cervix, move the cervix forward, and work with hormones to ripen and efface the cervix.
normal childbirth	Birth that occurs without complications or interventions, including medications.
obstetrician-gynecologist (ob-gyn)	A doctor who has additional training in women's health, pregnancy, birth, and postpartum. Ob-gyns focus on detecting and treating problems.
occiput	The back of the head.
occiput anterior (OA)	A fetal position in which the back of the baby's head lies against the mother's belly.
occiput posterior (OP)	A fetal position in which the back of the baby's head lies against the mother's back.
occiput transverse (OT)	A fetal position in which the back of the baby's head lies against the mother's side.
oligohydramnios	Low amniotic fluid.
osteopath	A doctor whose practice combines medical testing and treatment with hands-on diagnosis and treatment focusing on the muscles, bones, and nerves.
oxytocin	A hormone that stimulates uterine contractions and milk letdown.
pediatric or family nurse practitioner	A registered nurse with additional training in pediatrics or family health. Nurse practitioners treat common illnesses and provide well-child care.
pediatrician	A doctor who specializes in caring for children's health.
pelvic floor	The muscles between the pubic bone and the tailbone.
perinatologist	An ob-gyn with additional training in managing high-risk pregnancies and births.
perineal block	Anesthetic medication given to numb the perineum.
perineum	The tissues between the vagina and anus.
Pitocin	An artificial hormone that stimulates uterine contractions.
placenta	In pregnancy, an organ that allows the transfer of blood and nutrients from mother to fetus.
placenta accreta	Placenta growing into uterine muscle.
placenta previa	A placenta lying over or near the cervix.
placental abruption	Separation of the placenta from the uterus.
position	In pregnancy and labor, the direction in which the back of the baby's head is pointing.
positive affirmations	Repitition of optimistic statements as part of a ritual to help improve one's outlook.
postmaturity	A late-pregnancy condition in which the baby's growth slows down or stops, the placenta functions poorly, and the risk of fetal death rises.
postpartum doula	A person with training and experience in helping women and their families adjust to life with a new baby.
postpartum hemorrhage	Severe bleeding in the first twenty-four hours after birth.
postpartum mood disorders (PPMDs)	A family of mental health conditions that may begin any time during the first year postpartum and can last indefinitely without treatment. PPMDs occur more often in women who have a history of depression, anxiety, or psychological trauma.
postpartum psychosis	A rare and very serious postpartum mood disorder characterized by inability to sleep, severe agitation, mood swings, depression, or delusions. Postpartum psychosis usually appears soon after birth.
preeclampsia	A dangerous condition related to high blood pressure in pregnancy. Its symptoms include high blood pressure; protein in the urine; sudden swelling in the hands or face; rapid weight gain; headache; changes in or problems with vision; and pain in the stomach, the right side, the shoulder, or the lower back.
pregnancy-induced hypertension (PIH)	A condition in which a pregnant woman develops high blood pressure after twenty weeks gestation.
prelabor	The changes your body undergoes to prepare for labor. Prelabor may last anywhere from a few days to a few weeks.
presentation	In pregnancy and labor, the part of the baby's body lying over the cervix.

preterm labor	Labor contractions occurring before thirty-seven weeks LMP.
progressing contractions	Uterine contractions that grow stronger, longer, and more frequent over time to ripen, efface, and dilate the cervix as well as rotate and push the baby down and out of the uterus.
prostaglandin	A hormone that helps soften the cervix so it can efface and dilate.
rebozo	A traditional Mexican shawl used in labor to relieve back pain and improve a baby's position.
retained placenta	A postpartum condition in which placental fragments remain in the uterus.
ripening	Softening of the cervix so it can change shape during labor, expressed as firm, medium, or soft.
round ligaments	Muscular cords that connect the uterus with the groin tissues.
rupture of membranes (ROM)	Breaking open of amniotic sac, releasing amniotic fluid.
sacrum	A large, triangular bone at the base of the spine.
second stage of labor	The pushing stage of labor, which begins when the cervix is fully dilated and ends when the baby is born.
spinal block	A method of delivering medication into the lower back, near nerve roots in the spine. A caregiver administers a single injection of medication by inserting a needle into the intrathecal space.
splinting	Supporting a surgical incision by pressing gently on it with one's hand, a towel, or a pillow.
spontaneous pushing	A pushing method in which a mother pushes only when her body involuntarily bears down.
station	In pregnancy and labor, the vertical position of the baby in relation to the mother's pelvic bones.
sterile water block	A group of four small injections of sterile water into the lower back. The sterile water block relieves back pain by rapidly increasing endorphin production at the injection site.
stretch marks	Reddish lines appearing during pregnancy on expanding areas of skin, such as the abdomen, buttocks, breasts, thighs, or arms.
sudden infant death syndrome (SIDS)	Death of an apparently healthy infant, usually before one year of age, due to an unknown cause and occurring especially during sleep.
telemetry	Wireless electronic fetal monitoring.
third stage of labor	The delivery of the placenta during childbirth.
transcutaneous electrical nerve stimulation (TENS)	A device that delivers low-voltage electrical currents through the skin for pain relief.
transition	The final phase of the first stage of labor, beginning when the cervix dilates to about 8 centimeters and ending at 10 centimeters dilation.
transverse presentation	A fetal posture in which one shoulder lies over the cervix.
umbilical cord	A cord connecting a pregnant woman's placenta with the navel of her baby. The umbilical cord contains blood vessels that supply the fetus with oxygen and nutrients.
uterine hyperstimulation	Dangerously severe contractions; contractions that are too long, strong, or frequent.
uterine rupture	When the uterus tears open during labor.
uterus	A hollow, muscular organ shaped like an upside-down pear.
vaccine	A medication made from killed or weakened microbes that helps a person become immune to a disease without getting sick from it.
vacuum extractor	A silicone suction cup at the end of a long handle, used during childbirth to help the baby exit the mother's body.
varicose veins	Swollen, twisted blood vessels that bulge just beneath the skin.
vascular spider	Small central red bump with reddish legs stretching outward, caused when tiny blood vessels just under the skin dilate or burst.
vernix	Pasty protective coating on a fetus or newborn's skin.
vitamin K	A nutrient the human body needs in order for blood clotting to occur.
well-child visit	A health-care exam in which a caregiver checks a child's growth, development, and overall health and gives vaccinations as needed.

Recommended Resources

Books
Block, Jennifer. *Pushed: The Painful Truth About Childbirth and Modern Maternity Care*. Cambridge, MA: Da Capo, 2007.
Boston Women's Health Book Collective. *Our Bodies, Ourselves: Pregnancy and Birth*. New York: Touchstone, 2008.
Cox, Sue. *Breastfeeding with Confidence*. Minneapolis, MN: Meadowbrook, 2006.
Durham, Janelle. *Having a Baby: Your Personal Workbook*. Minneapolis, MN: Meadowbrook, 2006.
Giles, Fiona. *Fresh Milk: The Secret Life of Breasts*. New York: Simon and Schuster, 2003.
Goer, Henci. *The Thinking Woman's Guide to a Better Birth*. New York: Penguin, 1999.
La Leche League International. *The Womanly Art of Breastfeeding*. New York: Ballantine, 2010.
Lothian, Judith, and Charlotte DeVries. *The Official Lamaze Guide: Giving Birth with Confidence*. Minneapolis, MN: Meadowbrook, 2010.
Odes, Rebecca, and Ceridwen Morris. *From the Hips: A Comprehensive, Open-Minded, Uncensored, Totally Honest Guide to Pregnancy, Birth, and Becoming a Parent*. New York: Three Rivers Press, 2007.
Rapley, Gill, and Tracey Murkett. *Baby-Led Weaning: The Essential Guide to Introducing Solid Foods and Helping Your Baby to Grow Up a Happy and Confident Eater*. New York: The Experiment, 2010.
Sears, Martha and William. *The Baby Book: Everything You Need to Know About Your Baby from Birth to Age Two*. New York: Little, Brown, 2003.
Sears, Martha and William. *The Breastfeeding Book: Everything You Need to Know About Nursing Your Child from Birth Through Weaning*. New York: Little, Brown, 2000.
Sears, Robert. *The Vaccine Book: Making the Right Decision for Your Child*. New York: Little, Brown, 2007.
Simkin, Penny. *The Birth Partner*. Boston: Harvard Common Press, 2008.
Simkin, Penny, Janet Whalley, Ann Keppler, Janelle Durham, and April Bolding. *Pregnancy, Childbirth, and the Newborn*. Minneapolis, MN: Meadowbrook, 2010.
Simkin, Penny, Janet Whalley, and Ann Keppler. *The Simple Guide to Having a Baby*. Minneapolis, MN: Meadowbrook, 2005.
Swinney, Bridget. *Baby Bites*. Minneapolis, MN: Meadowbrook, 2007.
Swinney, Bridget. *Eating Expectantly: A Practical and Tasty Guide to Prenatal Nutrition*. Minneapolis, MN: Meadowbrook, 2000.
Wagner, Marsden. *Born in the USA: How a Broken Maternity System Must Be Fixed to Put Mothers and Infants First*. Berkeley, CA: University of California Press, 2006.
Wagner, Marsden. *Creating Your Birth Plan: The Definitive Guide to a Safe and Empowering Birth*. New York: Penguin, 2006.

Films
Being Dad: Inspiration and Information for Dads-To-Be. DVD. Westlake Village, CA: Seedsman Group, 2008.
Being Dad 2: Bringing the Baby Home. DVD. Westlake Village, CA: Seedsman Group, 2009.
Born in the USA: A Provocative Look at Having Babies in America. DVD. San Francisco: PatchWorks Films, 2000.
The Business of Being Born. DVD. New York: New Line Home Video, 2008.
Laugh and Learn About Childbirth. DVD. Norwalk, CT: Expect This LLC, 2007.
National Geographic: In the Womb. DVD. Washington, DC: National Geographic Video, 2006.
Orgasmic Birth. DVD. Westlake Village, CA: Seedsman Group, 2008.
With Woman: A Documentary About Women, Midwives, and Birth. DVD. Seattle, WA: CustomFlix, 2006.

Websites	
Baby-Friendly Hospital Initiative USA	http://www.babyfriendlyusa.org
Breastfeeding (Centers for Disease Control and Prevention)	http://www.cdc.gov/breastfeeding
Breastfeeding (United Nations Children's Fund)	http://www.unicef.org/nutrition/index_24824.html
Breastfeeding Committee for Canada	http://www.breastfeedingcanada.ca
Breastfeeding Initiatives (American Academy of Pediatrics)	http://www.aap.org/breastfeeding
Breastfeeding Laws (National Conference of State Legislatures)	http://www.ncsl.org/IssuesResearch/Health/BreastfeedingLaws/tabid/14389/Default.aspx
Caring for Kids (Canadian Paediatric Society)	http://www.cps.ca/caringforkids
Childbirth Connection	http://www.childbirthconnection.org

Continued on the next page

Continued from previous page

Websites	
Child Care Aware	http://www.childcareaware.org
Childcare (Babycenter)	http://www.babycenter.com/child-care
Citizens for Midwifery	http://cfmidwifery.org
Coalition for Improving Maternity Services (CIMS)	http://www.motherfriendly.org
Diaper Free Baby	http://www.diaperfreebaby.org
DONA International	http://www.dona.org
Donate Umbilical Cord Blood (National Marrow Donor Program)	http://www.marrow.org/HELP/Donate_Cord_Blood_Share_Life
Family Doctor (American Academy of Family Physicians)	http://www.familydoctor.org
Fathers' Forum Online	http://www.fathersforum.com
Got Mom (American College of Nurse-Midwives)	http://www.gotmom.org
Healthy Children (American Academy of Pediatrics)	http://www.healthychildren.org
Healthy Weight (Centers for Disease Control and Prevention)	http://www.cdc.gov/healthyweight
International Childbirth Education Association	http://www.icea.org
International Nanny Association	http://www.nanny.org
Kellymom: Breastfeeding & Parenting	http://www.kellymom.com
La Leche League International	http://www.llli.org
Lamaze International	http://www.lamaze.org
March of Dimes	http://www.marchofdimes.com
MomsRising	http://www.momsrising.org
Mothering	http://www.mothering.com
Mr. Dad	http://www.mrdad.com
My Midwife (American College of Nurse-Midwives)	http://www.mymidwife.org
National Association of Child Care Resource & Referral Agencies	http://www.naccrra.org
National Center on Shaken Baby Syndrome	http://www.dontshake.org
National Vaccine Information Center	http://www.nvic.org
Parent's Guide to Cord Blood Foundation	http://parentsguidecordblood.org
Patient Education Pamphlets (American Congress of Obstetrics and Gynecology)	http://www.acog.org/publications/patient_education
Postpartum Support International	http://postpartum.net
Preeclampsia Foundation	http://www.preeclampsia.org
Promoting Proper Feeding for Infants and Young Children (World Health Organization)	http://www.who.int/nutrition/topics/infantfeeding
Science & Sensibility	http://www.scienceandsensibility.org
Skin Deep Cosmetic Safety Database (Environmental Working Group)	http://www.cosmeticsdatabase.com
United States Breastfeeding Committee	http://www.usbreastfeeding.org
Vaccines & Immunizations (Centers for Disease Control and Prevention)	http://www.cdc.gov/vaccines
Women's Health Information (Society of Obstetricians and Gynaecologists of Canada)	http://www.sogc.org/health/index_e.asp
WorkOptions	http://workoptions.com

Index

Also from Meadowbrook Press

100,000+ Baby Names is the #1 baby name book and is the most complete guide for helping you name your baby. It contains more than 100,000 popular and unusual names from around the world, complete with origins, meanings, variations, and famous namesakes. It also includes the most recently available top 100 names for girls and boys, as well as over 300 helpful lists of names to consider and avoid.

Countdown to My Birth Experience pregnancy from your baby's point of view with this unique, award-winning, countdown calendar created by Julie B. Carr. This day-by-day account of pregnancy will help expecting mothers discover captivating facts, such as when the baby is the length and weight of a hot dog bun, when the heart begins to beat, and when the eyes open and look around. There are 280 daily developmental facts in all, beginning with "making me" and concluding with the "arrival."

Baby Play & Learn Child-development expert Penny Warner offers 160 ideas for games and activities that provide hours of developmental learning opportunities. It includes bulleted lists of skills baby learns through play, step-by-step instructions for each game and activity, and illustrations that demonstrate how to play many of the games.

Feed Me! I'm Yours is an easy-to-use, economical guide to making baby food at home. More than 200 recipes cover everything a parent needs to know about teething foods, nutritious snacks, and quick, pleasing lunches. Now recently revised.

First-Year Baby Care is one of the leading baby-care books to guide you through your baby's first year. It contains complete information on the basics of baby care, including bathing, diapering, medical facts, and feeding your baby. Now recently revised.

Baby & Child Emergency First Aid edited by Mitchell J. Einzig, MD. This user-friendly book is the next best thing to 911, with a quick-reference index, large illustrations, and easy-to-read instructions on handling the most common childhood emergencies.

We offer many more titles written to delight, inform, and entertain. To browse our full selection of titles, visit our web site at:

www.MeadowbrookPress.com

For quantity discounts, please call: 1-800-338-2232

Meadowbrook Press